T0037553

SUSAN SONTAG

On Women

Susan Sontag (1933–2004) was the author of numerous works of nonfiction, including the groundbreaking collection of essays *Against Interpretation*, and of four novels, including *In America*, which won the National Book Award.

Also by Susan Sontag

FICTION

The Benefactor

Death Kit

I, etcetera

The Way We Live Now

The Volcano Lover

In America

ESSAYS

Against Interpretation

Styles of Radical Will

On Photography

Illness as Metaphor

Under the Sign of Saturn

AIDS and Its Metaphors

Where the Stress Falls

Regarding the Pain of Others

At the Same Time

FILM SCRIPTS

Duet for Cannibals

Brother Carl

PLAY

Alice in Bed

JOURNALS

Reborn: Journals and Notebooks, 1947–1963

*As Consciousness Is Harnessed to Flesh:
Journals and Notebooks, 1964–1980*

ANTHOLOGY

A Susan Sontag Reader

On Women

On Women

SUSAN SONTAG

Edited by David Rieff

Introduction by Merve Emre

PICADOR

FARRAR, STRAUS AND GIROUX

New York

Picador
120 Broadway, New York 10271

Copyright © 2023 by The Estate of Susan Sontag
Introduction copyright © 2023 by Merve Emre
All rights reserved
Printed in the United States of America
First edition, 2023

Library of Congress Cataloging-in-Publication Data
Names: Sontag, Susan, 1933–2004, author. | Rieff, David, editor. |
    Emre, Merve, writer of introduction.
Title: On women / Susan Sontag ; edited by David Rieff ;
    introduction by Merve Emre.
Description: First edition. | New York : Picador, Farrar, Straus
    and Giroux 2023.
Identifiers: LCCN 2022059248 | ISBN 9781250876850 (paperback)
Subjects: LCGFT: Essays. | Interviews.
Classification: LCC PS3569.O6547 O5 2023 | DDC 814/.54—
    dc23/eng/20230125
LC record available at https://lccn.loc.gov/2022059248

Our books may be purchased in bulk for promotional,
educational, or business use. Please contact your local bookseller
or the Macmillan Corporate and Premium Sales Department
at 1-800-221-7945, extension 5442, or by email at
MacmillanSpecialMarkets@macmillan.com.

Picador® is a U.S. registered trademark and is used by Macmillan
Publishing Group, LLC, under license from Pan Books Limited.

For book club information, please visit facebook.com/picadorbookclub
or email marketing@picadorusa.com.

picadorusa.com • instagram.com/picador
twitter.com/picadorusa • facebook.com/picadorusa

10 9 8 7 6 5 4 3

CONTENTS

Introduction

by Merve Emre

A certain anxiety besieges the critic asked to introduce a volume of earlier writings on women, lest she should find the ideas expressed in them interesting only as relics of a distant, less enlightened past. What a relief it is to revisit the essays and interviews in Susan Sontag's *On Women* and to find them incapable of aging badly. It is true that the pieces are almost fifty years old, but far from prompting the gentle rebuke that they are "of their time," the effect of reading them today is to marvel at the untimeliness of their genius. They contain no ready-made ideas, no borrowed rhetoric—nothing that risks hardening into dogma or cant. They offer us only the spectacle of a ferocious intellect setting itself to the task at hand: to articulate the politics and aesthetics of being a woman in the United States, the Americas, and the world.

The singular glamour of Susan Sontag has done her some injustice, particularly where matters of sex and gender are concerned. Suspicious of her celebrity, convinced that her success had rendered her immune to the plights of ordinary women, her critics have characterized her relationship to the second sex as inconstant at best and faithless at worst. One can hardly miss the insinuation in, for instance, the poet and feminist activist Adrienne Rich's letter to *The New York Review of Books*, objecting to Sontag's essay on Leni Riefenstahl, "Fascinating Fascism." Dismissing Sontag's suggestion that feminists bore some responsibility for turning Riefenstahl's films into cultural monuments, Rich noted the "running criticism by radical feminists of male-identified 'successful' women, whether they are artists, executives, psychiatrists, Marxists, politicians, or scholars." It was no accident that, in Rich's letter, "male-identified" values extended beyond professional success to encompass the aesthetic and ethical phenomena that Sontag was drawn to in her writing: the metamorphosis of people into objects, the obliteration of personality by style, the pursuit of perfection through domination and submission—all painted with the same broad brush of patriarchy to indict the critic attracted to them.

We may agree with Rich that Sontag did not ally herself with the radical feminist movement. She questioned its inherited political rhetoric ("that of gauchisme," she wrote in her journal) and its dismissal of the intellect as "bourgeois, phallocentric, repressive." "Like all capital moral truths, feminism is a bit simple-minded," she observed in her response to Rich. Yet unless we consent to treating the moralizing rejection of "male-identified" women and values as a litmus test for what it means to be a feminist, we must remain skeptical of Rich's assertion that Sontag's writings on women were "more of an intellectual exercise than the expression of a felt reality—her own—interpreted by a keen mind."

In a journal entry from 1972, Sontag noted that "Women" was one of the three themes she had been following all her life, the other two being "China" and "Freaks." It was only in the 1970s, however, that the theme became central to her writing. The historical explanation is straightforward enough. The years from 1968 to 1973 were the most publicly visible and active stretch of the women's movement in the United States, years that appear to us now in an energetic sequence of film dissolves: women burning bras, women marching in the streets and swaying at candlelight vigils, women distributing mimeographed sheets with topics for consciousness raising, including equal pay, domestic violence, housework, childcare, and the right to an abortion; women thumbing through copies of *The Second Sex*, *The Feminine Mystique*, *The Dialectic of Sex*, and *Sexual Politics* with great intent. Nearly every notable woman essayist opined on the movement, often by assuming a tone of cool, disdainful skepticism toward its goals and principles. Today, one reads essays like Elizabeth Hardwick's curiously scattered "Women Re Women" or Joan Didion's vicious and startlingly shallow "The Women's Movement" with a vague sense of unease or, quite simply, bafflement at their authors' lack of fellow feeling, their lack of interest in the conditions that touched their lives as profoundly as the lives of women whom they condescended to so freely and gladly.

By contrast, Sontag's essays and interviews are forceful,

sympathetic, exceedingly truthful, and capacious in their imagination of what a woman is or could be. In a different world, *On Women* would have been the collection of essays that appeared between *Styles of Radical Will* (1969) and *Under the Sign of Saturn* (1980). The pieces gathered here represent an overlooked half decade of Sontag's writing, much of it undertaken between her trip to Vietnam and her first cancer diagnosis. Reading *On Women* in the context of both her individual history and history writ large, one realizes that the pieces in it were bracketed by death—that her entire notion of women was death-ridden, haunted by an awareness of mortality and the universal decline of the mind and body. "Thinking about my own death the other day, as I often do, I made a discovery," she wrote in her journal in 1974. "I realized that my way of thinking has up to now been both too abstract and too concrete. Too abstract: death. Too concrete: me. For there was a middle term, both abstract and concrete: women. I am a woman. And thereby, a whole new universe of death rose before my eyes." The specter of death spurred her to reconsider the relationship between the individual and the collective, between the lone woman and women as a historical category, capable of evolving and transforming over time. And she did so in a style that was more restrained and matter-of-fact than the flamboyant, belligerent beauty of her earlier essays, as if to speak of women as a whole required her, in part, to efface her exceptional self.

In the essays, death assumes many strange guises. Only rarely does it appear as she had imagined it would in her journal, in the gruesome forms of rape and murder and slavery. (A tantalizing journal entry contains notes for an essay she never wrote that she wanted to call "On Women Dying" or "How Women Die.") Sometimes, as in "The Third World of Women," her extraordinary 1972 interview with the leftist quarterly *Libre*, death was the will to self-annihilation of the entire global order, whose ideology of unlimited growth went hand in hand with "ever-increasing levels of productivity and consumption; the unlimited cannibalization of the environment." Women and men alike were ensnared by this naked, howling desire to accumulate more and more and more, but women were additionally oppressed by the institution of the nuclear family, "a prison of sexual repression, a playing field of inconsistent moral laxity, a museum of possessiveness, a guilt-producing factory, and a school of selfishness." The fact that the family was also the source of apparently unalienated values ("warmth, trust, dialogue, uncompetitiveness, loyalty, spontaneity, sexual pleasure, fun") only increased its power.

In articulating this double diagnosis, Sontag was careful to distance herself from the rhetoric of the socialist or Marxist feminists of the era; there is, throughout the interview, a noticeable allergy to political radicalism and a deep conviction that work may be a source of pride, affirmation, and justifiable social and cultural distinction. Yet she understood as well as these feminists did that the integrity of the family depended on the exploitation of women's unwaged, domestic labor, and on devaluing this labor as playing nothing other than a "supportive, backup role in the economy." "Women who have gained the freedom to go out into 'the world' but still have the responsibility for marketing, cooking, cleaning, and the children when they return from work have simply doubled their labor," she insisted. Liberation from death into life required a revolution that would overthrow the desire to accrete capital and the authoritarian moral habits that kept the division of labor—men at work, women in the home—intact.

Most often, however, death appeared in these essays as the slow erosion of one's sense of self and the painful contraction of life's possibilities. Sontag described it with terrible clarity and frankness in "The Double Standard of Aging." "Growing older is mainly an ordeal of the imagination—a moral disease, a social pathology—intrinsic to which is the fact that it afflicts women much more than men," she wrote. Day by day, the horizons of one's possibilities dimmed and receded. The body began to bear the signs of its diminishment; it was exposed as the most intimate traitor to the vision of the firm, unlined self that was forged in youth. Yet the vision was itself traitorous to women, Sontag insisted. "Beauty, women's business in this society, is the theater of their enslavement. Only one standard of female beauty is sanctioned: the *girl*." Women were not permitted to change, were not allowed to cast off their smooth innocence and docility in favor of wisdom, competence, strength, and ambition without fear of social recrimination. The essays in *On Women* make clear that, for her, the oppression of women presented an aesthetic and narrative problem as well as a political and economic one.

Does beauty pose a problem for feminism? Perhaps the better question to ask of Sontag's essays is: Does beauty pose a problem for how women imagine their futures? What would it mean to be liberated from beauty's conventional images, its stock stories? It is always a little embarrassing for a beautiful woman to write about physical beauty, for she finds she must serve as both the subject and the object of her judgments. But it is just as embarrassing, if not more, for her to admit that her beauty has started to crumple, to fade; for her beauty to define her now not by its startling presence, but by its absence. Sontag was thirty-nine, on the cusp of forty, when she wrote "The Double Standard of Aging"—one of the only personal details she reveals throughout *On Women*. She was in her early forties when she wrote the two short essays on beauty, "A Woman's Beauty: Put-Down or Power Source?" and "Beauty: How Will It Change Next?" "To be sure, beauty is a form of power. And deservedly so," she wrote. Yet it was a power that had always been conceived in relation to men: "not the power to do but the power to attract." "It is a power that negates itself. For this power is not one that can be chosen freely—at least, not by women—or renounced without social censure."

In her quest to place women in a fresher and more empowered relation to beauty, she was aided by her long-standing suspicion of beauty as a judgment of both people and artworks. It was a suspicion she first aired formally in *Notes on "Camp,"* in which she implied that the alliance brokered between beauty and mass civilization had authorized a certain tedium and predictability of taste. In *On Women*, that alliance helped to secure the oppression of women by holding them to standards of self-presentation that are at once too flexible, too quick to essentialize the whims of the market and its aesthetic values; and too rigid, incapable of bestowing social recognition upon those who were old, loud, ugly, unfeminine, disabled. If, as she argued, beauty had been "abridged in order to prop up the mythology of the 'feminine,'" then a more shocking and forgiving definition of beauty required unsexing it, violently. Beauty would no longer be subject to the approval of men; it would appropriate the masculine to do women's bidding for them.

Camp is the hidden nerve running through the essays in *On Women*. Initially conceived of by Sontag as apolitical, in these essays, it emerges the privileged sensibility of a politics of feminist liberation. If camp meant going against the grain of one's sex by engaging in a "robust, shrill, vulgar parody" of gender, as she described it in her interview with *Salmagundi* magazine, then there is something fantastically campy in her imagination of the politics of consciousness raising. She encouraged women to think of themselves as actors in a "guerrilla theater" or revolution, in which they would perform the following acts in the most exaggerated and contemptuous manner possible:

They should whistle at men in the streets, raid beauty parlors, picket toy manufacturers who produce sexist toys, convert in sizeable numbers to militant lesbianism, operate their own free psychiatric and abortion clinics, provide feminist divorce counseling, establish makeup withdrawal centers, adopt their mothers' family names as their last names, deface billboard advertising that insults women, disrupt public events by singing in honor of the docile wives of male celebrities and politicians, collect pledges to renounce alimony and giggling, bring lawsuits for defamation against the mass-circulation "women's magazines," conduct telephone harassment campaigns against male psychiatrists who have sexual relations with their women patients, organize beauty contests for men, put up feminist candidates for all public offices.

"Women will be much more effective politically if they are rude, shrill, and—by sexist standards—'unattractive,'" she proposed. "They will be met with ridicule, which they should do more than bear stoically. They should, indeed, welcome it." Welcoming it helped neutralize the sexist condemnation of men. But it was also the first step toward eradicating the ideological division of men and women along lines of sex—for her, the ultimate end of feminist revolution. "A society in which women are subjectively and objectively the genuine equals of men . . . will necessarily be an androgynous society." She did not value separatism, the aggressive policing of the boundaries of who was or was not a woman, what was or was not beautiful. She valued the blatant disorganization of gender and sexuality and the individual's right to plural forms of being; her right to her many fractured selves. She envisioned an aesthetic and political integration of men and women that would, in the final analysis, result in the obliteration of both categories of identity. Then there would be no need for women to establish for themselves a private culture, no need for them to seek rooms of their own. "It's just that they should be seeking to abolish," she concluded.

It is the interviews that stand out to me as the secret treasures of *On Women* and of Sontag's oeuvre in general, for it is the interviews that make the most space for a plurality of style and thought that mirrored her belief in the plurality of the self. "To be an intellectual is to be attached to the inherent value of plurality, and to the right of critical space (space for critical opposition within society)," she wrote in her journal. One finds in the interviews a voice that is rigorous still, but bolder and freer and more gladiatorial in its pronouncements. We hear, once more, the eager combativeness of her earlier essays. We hear, too, her willingness to respond, challenge, qualify, speculate; her refusal of easy answers or offended pieties. We feel the hunger that drove her to keep thinking. And we feel, across the great and growing distance of time, the force of her demand that we never stop thinking alongside her.

On Women

The Double Standard of Aging

"How old are you?" The person asking the question is anybody. The respondent is a woman, a woman "of a certain age," as the French say discreetly. That age might be anywhere from her early twenties to her late fifties. If the question is impersonal—routine information requested when she applies for a driver's license, a credit card, a passport—she will probably force herself to answer truthfully. Filling out a marriage license application, if her future husband is even slightly her junior, she may long to subtract a few years; probably she won't. Competing for a job, her chances often partly depend on being the "right age," and if hers isn't right, she will lie if she thinks she can get away with it. Making her first visit to a new doctor, perhaps feeling particularly vulnerable at the moment she's asked, she will probably hurry through the correct answer. But if the question is only what people call personal—if she's asked by a new friend, a casual acquaintance, a neighbor's child, a coworker in an office, store, factory—her response is harder to predict. She may sidestep the question with a joke or refuse it with playful indignation. "Don't you know you're not supposed to ask a woman her age?" Or, hesitating a moment, embarrassed but defiant, she may tell the truth. Or she may lie. But neither truth, evasion, nor lie relieves the unpleasantness of that question. For a woman to be obliged to state her age, after "a certain age," is always a miniature ordeal.

If the question comes from a woman, she will feel less threatened than if it comes from a man. Other women are, after all, comrades in sharing the same potential for humiliation. She will be less arch, less coy. But she probably still dislikes answering and may not tell the truth. Bureaucratic formalities excepted, whoever asks a woman this question—after "a certain age"—is ignoring a taboo and possibly being impolite or downright hostile. Almost everyone acknowledges that once she passes an age that is, actually, quite young, a woman's exact age ceases to be a legitimate target of curiosity. After childhood the year of a woman's birth becomes her secret, her private property. It is something of a dirty secret. To answer truthfully is always indiscreet.

The discomfort a woman feels each time she tells her age is quite independent of the anxious awareness of human mortality that everyone has, from time to time. There is a normal sense in which nobody, men and women alike, relishes growing older. After thirty-five any mention of one's age carries with it the reminder that one is probably closer to the end of one's life than to the beginning. There is nothing unreasonable in that anxiety. Nor is there any abnormality in the anguish and anger that

4

people who are really old, in their seventies and eighties, feel about the implacable waning of their powers, physical and mental. Advanced age is undeniably a trial, however stoically it may be endured. It is a shipwreck, no matter with what courage elderly people insist on continuing the voyage. But the objective, sacred pain of old age is of another order than the subjective, profane pain of aging. Old age is a genuine ordeal, one that men and women undergo in a similar way. Growing older is mainly an ordeal of the imagination—a moral disease, a social pathology—intrinsic to which is the fact that it afflicts women much more than men. It is particularly women who experience growing older (everything that comes *before* one is actually old) with such distaste and even shame.

The emotional privileges this society confers upon youth stir up some anxiety about getting older in everybody. All modern urbanized societies—unlike tribal, rural societies—condescend to the values of maturity and heap honors on the joys of youth. This revaluation of the life cycle in favor of the young brilliantly serves a secular society whose idols are ever-increasing industrial productivity and the unlimited cannibalization of nature. Such a society must create a new sense of the rhythms of life in order to incite people to buy more, to consume and throw away faster. People let the direct awareness they have of their needs, of what really gives them pleasure, be overruled by commercialized *images* of happiness and personal well-being; and, in this imagery designed to stimulate ever more avid levels of consumption, the most popular metaphor for happiness is "youth." (I would insist that it is a metaphor, not a literal description. Youth is a metaphor for energy, restless mobility, appetite: for the state of "wanting.") This equating of well-being with youth makes everyone naggingly aware of exact age—one's own and that of other people. In primitive and premodern societies people attach much less importance to dates. When lives are divided into long periods with stable responsibilities and steady ideals (and hypocrisies), the exact number of years someone has lived becomes a trivial fact; there is hardly any reason to mention, even to know, the year in which one was born. Most people in nonindustrial societies are not sure exactly how old they are. People in industrial societies are haunted by numbers. They take an almost obsessional interest in keeping the scorecard of aging, convinced that anything above a low total is some kind of bad news. In an era in which people actually live longer and longer, what now amounts to the latter *two-thirds* of everyone's life is shadowed by a poignant apprehension of unremitting loss.

The prestige of youth afflicts everyone in this society to some degree. Men, too, are prone to periodic bouts of depression about aging—for instance, when feeling insecure or unfulfilled or insufficiently rewarded in their jobs. But men rarely panic about aging in the way women often do. Getting older is less profoundly wounding for a man, for in addition to the propaganda for youth that puts both men and women on the defensive as they age, there is a double standard about aging that denounces women with special severity. Society is much more permissive about aging in men, as it is more tolerant of the sexual infidelities of husbands. Men are "allowed" to age, without penalty, in several ways that women are not.

This society offers even fewer rewards for aging women than it does to men. Being physically attractive counts much more in a woman's life than in a man's, but beauty, identified, as it is for women, with youthfulness, does not stand up well to age. Exceptional mental powers can increase with age, but women are rarely encouraged to develop their minds above dilettante standards. Because the wisdom considered the special province of women is "eternal," an age-old, intuitive knowledge about the emotions to which a repertoire of facts, worldly experience, and the methods of rational analysis have nothing to contribute, living a long time does not promise women an increase in wisdom either. The private skills expected of women are exercised early and, with the exception of a talent for making love, are not the kind that enlarge with experience. "Masculinity" is identified with competence, autonomy, self-control—qualities which the disappearance of youth does not threaten. Competence in most of the activities expected from men, physical sports excepted, increases with age. "Femininity" is identified with incompetence, helplessness, passivity, noncompetitiveness, being nice. Age does not improve these qualities.

Middle-class men feel diminished by aging, even while still young, if they have not yet shown distinction in their careers or made a lot of money. (And any tendencies they have toward hypochondria will get worse in middle age, focusing with particular nervousness on the specter of heart attacks and the loss of virility.) Their aging crisis is linked to that terrible pressure on men to be "successful" that precisely defines their membership in the middle class. Women rarely feel anxious about their age because they haven't succeeded at something. The work that women do outside the home rarely counts as a form of achievement, only as a way of earning money; most employment available to women mainly exploits the training they have been receiving since early childhood to be servile, to be both supportive and parasitical, to be unadventurous. They can have menial, low-skilled jobs in light industries, which offer as feeble a criterion of success as housekeeping. They can be secretaries, clerks, sales personnel, maids, research assistants, waitresses, social workers, prostitutes, nurses, teachers, telephone operators—public transcriptions of the servicing and nurturing roles that women have in family life. Women fill very few executive posts, are rarely found suitable for large corporate or political responsibilities, and form only a tiny contingent in the liberal professions (apart from teaching). They are virtually barred from jobs that involve an expert, intimate relation with machines or an aggressive use of the body, or that carry any physical risk or sense of adventure. The jobs this society deems appropriate to women are auxiliary, "calm" activities that do not compete with, but aid, what men do. Besides being less well paid, most work women do has a lower ceiling of advancement and gives meager outlet to normal wishes to be powerful. All outstanding work by women in this society is voluntary; most women are too inhibited by the social disapproval attached to their being ambitious and aggressive. Inevitably, women are exempted from the dreary panic of middle-aged men whose "achievements" seem paltry, who feel stuck on the job ladder or fear being pushed off it by someone younger. But they are also denied most of the real satisfactions that men derive from work—satisfactions that often do increase with age.

The double standard about aging shows up most brutally in the conventions of sexual feeling, which presuppose a disparity between men and women that operates permanently to women's disadvantage. In the accepted course of events a woman anywhere from her late teens through her middle twenties can expect to attract a man more or less her own age. (Ideally, he should be at least slightly older.) They marry and raise a family. But if her husband starts an affair after some years of marriage, he customarily does so with a woman much younger than his wife. Suppose, when both husband and wife are already in their late forties or early fifties, they divorce. The husband has an excellent chance of getting married again, probably to a younger woman. His ex-wife finds it difficult to re-marry. Attracting a second husband younger than herself is improbable; even to find someone her own age she has to be lucky, and she will probably have to settle for a man considerably older than herself, in his sixties or seventies. Women become sexually ineligible much earlier than men do. A man, even an ugly man, can remain eligible well into old age. He is an acceptable mate for a young, attractive woman. Women, even good-looking women, become ineligible (except as partners of very old men) at a much younger age.

Thus, for most women, aging means a humiliating process of gradual sexual disqualification. Since women are considered maximally eligible in early youth, after which their sexual value drops steadily, even young women feel themselves in a desperate race against the calendar. They are old as soon as they are no longer very young. In late adolescence some girls are already worrying about getting married. Boys and young men have little reason to anticipate trouble because of aging. What makes men desirable to women is by no means tied to youth. On the contrary, getting older tends (for several decades) to operate in men's favor, since their value as lovers and husbands is set more by what they do than how they look. Many men have more success romantically at forty than they did at twenty or twenty-five; fame, money, and, above all, power are sexually enhancing. (A woman who has won power in a competitive profession or business career is considered less, rather than more, desirable. Most men confess themselves intimidated or turned off sexually by such a woman, obviously because she is harder to treat as just a sexual "object.") As they age, men may start feeling anxious about actual sexual performance, worrying about a loss of sexual vigor or even impotence, but their sexual eligibility is not abridged simply by getting older. Men stay sexually possible as long as they can make love. Women are at a disadvantage because their sexual candidacy depends on meeting certain much stricter "conditions" related to looks and age.

Since women are imagined to have much more limited sexual lives than men do, a woman who has never married is pitied. She was not found acceptable, and it is assumed that her life continues to confirm her unacceptability. Her presumed lack of sexual opportunity is embarrassing. A man who remains a bachelor is judged much less crudely. It is assumed that he, at any age, still has a sexual life—or the chance of one. For men there is no destiny equivalent to the humiliating condition of being an old maid, a spinster. "Mr.," a cover from infancy to senility, precisely exempts men from the stigma that attaches to any woman, no longer young, who is still "Miss." (That women are divided into "Miss" and "Mrs.," which calls unrelenting attention to the situation of each woman with respect to marriage, reflects the belief that being single or married is much more decisive for a woman than it is for a man.)

For a woman who is no longer very young, there is certainly some relief when she has finally been able to marry. Marriage soothes the sharpest pain she feels about the passing years. But her anxiety never subsides completely, for she knows that should she reenter the sexual market at a later date—because of divorce, or the death of her husband, or the need for erotic adventure—she must do so under a handicap far greater than any man of her age (*whatever* her age may be) and regardless of how good-looking she is. Her achievements, if she has a career, are no asset. The calendar is the final arbiter.

To be sure, the calendar is subject to some variations from country to country. In Spain, Portugal, and the Latin American countries, the age at which most women are ruled physically undesirable comes earlier than in the United States. In France it is somewhat later. French conventions of sexual feeling make a quasi-official place for the woman between thirty-five and forty-five. Her role is to initiate an inexperienced or timid young man, after which she is, of course, replaced by a young girl. (Colette's novella *Chéri* is the best-known account in fiction of such a love affair; biographies of Balzac relate a well-documented example from real life.) This sexual myth does make turning forty somewhat easier for French women. But there is no difference in any of these countries in the basic attitudes that disqualify women sexually much earlier than men.

Aging also varies according to social class. Poor people look old much earlier in their lives than do rich people. But anxiety about aging is certainly more common, and more acute, among middle-class and rich women than among working-class women. Economically disadvantaged women in this society are more fatalistic about aging; they can't afford to fight the cosmetic battle as long or as tenaciously. Indeed, nothing so clearly indicates the fictional nature of this crisis than the fact that women who keep their youthful appearance the longest—women who lead unstrenuous, physically sheltered lives, who eat balanced meals, who can afford good medical care, who have few or no children—are those who feel the defeat of age most keenly. Aging is much more a social judgment than a biological eventuality. Far more extensive than the hard sense of loss suffered during menopause (which, with increased longevity, tends to arrive later and later) is the depression about aging, which may not be set off by any real event in a woman's life, but is a recurrent state of "possession" of her imagination, ordained by society—that is, ordained by the way this society limits how women feel free to imagine themselves.

There is a model account of the aging crisis in Richard Strauss's sentimental-ironic opera *Der Rosenkavalier*, whose heroine is a wealthy and glamorous married woman who decides to renounce romance. After a night with her adoring young lover, the Marschallin has a sudden, unexpected confrontation with herself. It is toward the end of Act I; Octavian has just left. Alone in her bedroom she sits at her dressing table, as she does every morning. It is the daily ritual of self-appraisal practiced by every woman. She looks at herself and, appalled, begins to weep. Her youth is over. Note that the Marschallin does not discover, looking in the mirror, that she is ugly. She is as beautiful as ever. The Marschallin's discovery is moral—that is, it is a discovery of her imagination; it is nothing she actually *sees*. Nevertheless, her discovery is no less devastating. Bravely, she makes her painful, gallant decision. She will arrange for her beloved Octavian to fall in love with a girl his own age. She must be realistic. She is no longer eligible. She is now "the old Marschallin."

Strauss wrote the opera in 1910. Contemporary opera-goers are rather shocked when they discover that the libretto indicates that the Marschallin is all of thirty-four years old; today the role is generally sung by a soprano well into her forties or in her fifties. Acted by an attractive singer of thirty-four, the Marschallin's sorrow would seem merely neurotic, or even ridiculous. Few women today think of themselves as old, wholly disqualified from romance, at thirty-four. The age of retirement has moved up, in line with the sharp rise in life expectancy for everybody in the last few generations. The *form* in which women experience their lives remains unchanged. A moment approaches inexorably when they must resign themselves to being "too old." And that moment is invariably—objectively—premature.

In earlier generations the renunciation came even sooner. Fifty years ago a woman of forty was not just aging but old, finished. No struggle was even possible. Today, the surrender to aging no longer has a fixed date. The aging crisis (I am speaking only of women in affluent countries) starts earlier but lasts longer; it is diffused over most of a woman's life. A woman hardly has to be anything like what would reasonably be considered old to worry about her age, to start lying (or being tempted to lie). The crises can come at any time. Their schedule depends on a blend of personal ("neurotic") vulnerability and the swing of social mores. Some women don't have their first crisis until thirty. No one escapes a sickening shock upon turning forty. Each birthday, but especially those ushering in a new decade—for round numbers have a special authority—sounds a new defeat. There is almost as much pain in the anticipation as in the reality. Twenty-nine has become a queasy age ever since the official end of youth crept forward, about a generation ago, to thirty. Being thirty-nine is also hard; a whole year in which to meditate in glum astonishment that one stands on the threshold of middle age. The frontiers are arbitrary, but not any less vivid for that. Although a woman on her fortieth birthday is hardly different from what she was when she was still thirty-nine, the day seems like a turning point. But long before actually becoming a woman of forty, she has been steeling herself against the depression she will feel. One of the greatest tragedies of each woman's life is simply getting older; it is certainly the *longest* tragedy.

Aging is a movable doom. It is a crisis that never exhausts itself, because the anxiety is never really used up. Being a crisis of the imagination rather than of "real life," it has the habit of repeating itself again and again. The territory of aging (as opposed to actual old age) has no fixed boundaries. Up to a point it can be defined as one wants. Entering each decade—after the initial shock is absorbed—an endearing, desperate impulse of survival helps many women to stretch the boundaries to the decade following. In late adolescence thirty seems the end of life. At thirty, one pushes the sentence forward to forty. At forty, one still gives oneself ten more years.

I remember my closest friend in college sobbing on the day she turned twenty-one. "The best part of my life is over. I'm not young anymore." She was a senior, nearing graduation. I was a precocious freshman, just sixteen. Mystified, I tried lamely to comfort her, saying that I didn't think twenty-one was *so* old. Actually, I didn't understand at all what could be demoralizing about turning twenty-one. To me, it meant only something good: being in charge of oneself, being free. At sixteen, I was too young to have noticed, and become confused by, the peculiarly loose, ambivalent way in which this society demands that one stop thinking of oneself as a girl and start thinking of oneself as a woman. (In America that demand can now be put off to the age of thirty, even beyond.) But even if I thought her distress was absurd, I must have been aware that it would not simply be absurd but quite unthinkable in a *boy* turning twenty-one. Only women worry about age with that degree of inanity and pathos. And, of course, as with all crises that are inauthentic and therefore repeat themselves compulsively (because the danger is largely fictive, a poison in the imagination), this friend of mine went on having the same crisis over and over, each time as if for the first time.

I also came to her thirtieth birthday party. A veteran of many love affairs, she had spent most of her twenties living abroad and had just returned to the United States.

She had been good-looking when I first knew her; now she was beautiful. I teased her about the tears she had shed over being twenty-one. She laughed and claimed not to remember. But thirty, she said ruefully, that really is the end. Soon after, she married. My friend is now forty-four. While no longer what people call beautiful, she is striking-looking, charming, and vital. She teaches elementary school; her husband, who is twenty years older than she, is a part-time merchant seaman. They have one child, now nine years old. Sometimes, when her husband is away, she takes a lover. She told me recently that forty was the most upsetting birthday of all (I wasn't at that one), and although she has only a few years left, she means to enjoy them while they last. She has become one of those women who seize every excuse offered in any conversation for mentioning how old they really are, in a spirit of bravado compounded with self-pity that is not too different from the mood of women who regularly lie about their age. But she is actually fretting much less about aging than she was two decades ago. Having a child, and having one rather late, past the age of thirty, has certainly helped to reconcile her to her age. At fifty, I suspect, she will be ever more valiantly postponing the age of resignation.

My friend is one of the more fortunate, sturdier casualties of the aging crisis. Most women are not as spirited, nor as innocently comic in their suffering. But almost all women endure some version of this suffering: a recurrent seizure of the imagination that usually begins quite young, in which they project themselves into a calculation of loss. The rules of this society are cruel to women. Brought up to be never fully adult, women are deemed obsolete earlier than men. In fact most women don't become relatively free and expressive sexually until their thirties. (Women mature sexually this late, certainly much later than men, not for innate biological reasons but because this culture retards women. Denied most outlets for sexual energy permitted to men, it takes many women *that* long to wear out some of their inhibitions.) The time at which they start being disqualified as sexually attractive persons is just when they have grown up sexually. The double standard about aging cheats women of those years, between thirty-five and fifty, likely to be the best of their sexual life.

That women expect to be flattered often by men, and the extent to which their self-confidence depends on this flattery, reflects how deeply women are psychologically weakened by this double standard. Added on to the pressure felt by everybody in this society to look young as long as possible are the values of "femininity," which specifically identify sexual attractiveness in women with youth. The desire to be the "right age" has a special urgency for a woman it never has for a man. A much greater part of her self-esteem and pleasure in life is threatened when she ceases to be young. Most men experience getting older with regret, apprehension. But most women experience it even more painfully: with shame. Aging is a man's destiny, something that must happen because he is a human being. For a woman, aging is not only her destiny. Because she is that more *narrowly* defined kind of human being, a woman, it is also her vulnerability.

To be a woman is to be an actress. Being feminine is a kind of theater, with its appropriate costumes, décor, lighting, and stylized gestures. From early childhood on, girls are trained to care in a pathologically exaggerated way about their appearance and are profoundly mutilated (to the extent of being unfitted for first-class adulthood) by the extent of the stress put on presenting themselves as physically attractive objects. Women look in the mirror more frequently than men do. It is, virtually, their duty to look at themselves—to look often. Indeed, a woman who is not narcissistic is considered unfeminine. And a woman who spends literally *most* of her time caring for, and making purchases to flatter, her physical appearance is not regarded in this society as what she is: a kind of moral idiot. She is thought to be quite normal and is envied by other women whose time is mostly used up at jobs or caring for large families. The display of narcissism goes on all the time. It is expected that women will disappear several times in an evening—at a restaurant, at a party, during a theater intermission, in the course of a social visit—simply to check their appearance, to see that nothing has gone wrong with their makeup and hairstyling, to make sure that their clothes are not spotted or too wrinkled or not hanging properly. It is even acceptable to perform this activity in public. At the table in a restaurant, over coffee, a woman opens a compact mirror and touches up her makeup and hair without embarrassment in front of her husband or her friends.

All this behavior, which is written off as normal "vanity" in women, would seem ludicrous in a man. Women are more vain than men because of the relentless pressure on women to maintain their appearance at a certain high standard. What makes the pressure even more burdensome is that there are actually several standards. Men present themselves as face-and-body, a physical whole. Women are split, as men are not, into a body and a face—each judged by somewhat different standards. What is important for a face is that it be beautiful. What is important for a body is two things, which may even be (depending on fashion and taste) somewhat incompatible: first, that it be desirable and, second, that it be beautiful. Men usually feel sexually attracted to women much more because of their bodies than their faces. The traits that arouse desire— such as fleshiness—don't always match those that fashion decrees as beautiful. (For instance, the ideal woman's body promoted in advertising in recent years is extremely thin: the kind of body that looks more desirable clothed than naked.) But women's concern with their appearance is not simply geared to arousing desire in men. It also aims at fabricating a certain image by which, as a more indirect way of arousing desire, women state their value. A woman's value lies in the way she *represents* herself, which is much more by her face than her body. In defiance of the laws of simple sexual attraction, women do not devote most of their attention to their bodies. The well-known "normal" narcissism that women display—the amount of time they spend before the mirror—is used primarily in caring for the face and hair.

Women do not simply have faces, as men do; they are identified with their faces. Men have a naturalistic relation to their faces. Certainly they care whether they are good-looking or not. They suffer over acne, protruding ears, tiny eyes; they hate getting bald. But there is a much wider latitude in what is aesthetically acceptable in a man's face than what is in a woman's. A man's face is defined as something he basically doesn't need to tamper with; all he has to do is keep it clean. He can avail himself of the options for ornament supplied by nature: a beard, a mustache, longer or shorter hair. But he is not supposed to disguise himself. What he is "really" like is supposed to show. A man lives through his face; it records the progressive stages of his life. And since he doesn't tamper with his face, it is not separate from but is completed by his body—which is judged attractive by the impression it gives of virility and energy. By contrast, a woman's face is potentially separate from her body. She does not treat it naturalistically. A woman's face is the canvas upon which she paints a revised, corrected portrait of herself. One of the rules of this creation is that the face *not* show what she doesn't want it to show. Her face is an emblem, an icon, a flag. How she arranges her hair, the type of makeup she uses, the quality of her complexion—all these are signs, not of what she is "really" like, but of how she asks to be treated by others, especially men. They establish her status as an "object."

For the normal changes that age inscribes on every human face, women are much more heavily penalized than men. Even in early adolescence, girls are cautioned to protect their faces against wear and tear. Mothers tell their daughters (but never their sons): You look ugly when you cry. Stop worrying. Don't read too much. Crying, frowning, squinting, even laughing—all these human activities make "lines." The same usage of the face in men is judged quite positively. In a man's face lines are taken to be signs of "character." They indicate emotional strength, maturity— qualities far more esteemed in men than in women. (They show he has "lived.") Even scars are often not felt to be unattractive; they too can add "character" to a man's face. But lines of aging, any scar, even a small birthmark on a woman's face, are always regarded as unfortunate blemishes. In effect, people take character in men to be different from what constitutes character in women. A woman's character is thought to be innate, static—not the product of her experience, her years, her actions. A woman's face is prized so far as it remains unchanged by (or conceals the traces of) her emotions, her physical risk-taking. Ideally, it is supposed to be a mask—immutable, unmarked. The model woman's face is Garbo's. Because women are identified with their faces much more than men are, and the ideal woman's face is one that is "perfect," it seems a calamity when a woman has a disfiguring accident. A broken nose or a scar or a burn mark, no more than regrettable for a man, is a terrible psychological wound to a woman; objectively, it diminishes her value. (As is well known, most clients for plastic surgery are women.)

Both sexes aspire to a physical ideal, but what is expected of boys and what is expected of girls involves a very different moral relation to the self. Boys are encouraged to *develop* their bodies, to regard the body as an instrument to be improved. They invent their masculine selves largely through exercise and sport, which harden the body and strengthen competitive feelings; clothes are of only secondary help in making their bodies attractive. Girls are not particularly encouraged to develop their bodies through any activity, strenuous or not; and physical strength and endurance are hardly valued at all. The invention of the feminine self proceeds mainly through clothes and other signs that testify to the very effort of girls to look attractive, to their commitment to please. When boys become men, they may go on (especially if they have sedentary jobs) practicing a sport or doing exercises for a while. Mostly they leave their appearance alone, having been trained to accept more or less what nature has handed out to them. (Men may start doing exercises again in their forties to lose weight, but for reasons of health—there is an epidemic fear of heart attacks among the middle-aged in rich countries—not for cosmetic reasons.) As one of the norms of "femininity" in this society is being preoccupied with one's physical appearance, so "masculinity" means *not* caring very much about one's looks.

This society allows men to have a much more affirmative relation to their bodies than women have. Men are more "at home" in their bodies, whether they treat them casually or use them aggressively. A man's body is defined as a strong body. It contains no contradiction between what is felt to be attractive and what is practical. A woman's body, so far as it is considered attractive, is defined as a fragile, light body. (Thus, women worry more than men do about being overweight.) When they do exercises, women avoid the ones that develop the muscles, particularly those in the upper arms. Being "feminine" means looking physically weak, frail. Thus, the ideal woman's body is one that is not of much practical use in the hard work of this world, and one that must continually "be defended." Women do not develop their bodies, as men do. After a woman's body has reached its sexually acceptable form by late adolescence, most further development is viewed as negative. And it is thought irresponsible for women to do what is normal for men: simply leave their appearance alone. During early youth they are likely to come as close as they ever will to the ideal image—slim figure, smooth firm skin, light musculature, graceful movements. Their task is to try to maintain that image, unchanged, as long as possible. Improvement as such is not the task. Women care for their bodies—against toughening, coarsening, getting fat. They *conserve* them. (Perhaps the fact that women in modern societies tend to have a more conservative political outlook than men originates in their profoundly conservative relation to their bodies.)

In the life of women in this society the period of pride, of natural honesty, of unselfconscious flourishing is brief. Once past youth, women are condemned to inventing (and maintaining) themselves against the inroads of age. Most of the physical qualities regarded as attractive in women deteriorate much earlier in life than those defined as "male." Indeed, they perish fairly soon in the normal sequence of body transformation. The "feminine" is smooth, rounded, hairless, unlined, soft, unmuscled—the look of the very young; characteristics of the weak, of the vulnerable; eunuch traits, as Germaine Greer has pointed out. Actually, there are only a few years—late adolescence, early twenties—in which this look is physiologically natural, in which it can be had without touching-up and covering-up. After that, women enlist in a quixotic enterprise, trying to close the gap between the imagery put forth by society (concerning what is attractive in a woman) and the evolving facts of nature.

Women have a more intimate relation to aging than men do, simply because one of the accepted "women's" occupations is taking pains to keep one's face and body from showing the signs of growing older. Women's sexual validity depends, up to a certain point, on how well they stand off these natural changes. After late adolescence women become the caretakers of their bodies and faces, pursuing an essentially defensive strategy, a holding operation. A vast array of products in jars and tubes, a branch of surgery, and armies of hairdressers, masseuses, diet counselors, and other professionals exist to stave off, or mask, developments that are entirely normal biologically. Large amounts of women's energies are diverted into this passionate, corrupting effort to defeat nature: to maintain an ideal, static appearance against the progress of age. The collapse of the project is only a matter of time. Inevitably, a woman's physical appearance develops beyond its youthful form. No matter how exotic the creams or how strict the diets, one cannot indefinitely keep the face unlined, the waist slim. Bearing children takes its toll: the torso becomes thicker; the skin is stretched. There is no way to keep certain lines from appearing, in one's midtwenties, around the eyes and mouth. From about thirty on, the skin gradually loses its tonus. In women this perfectly natural process is regarded as a humiliating defeat, while nobody finds anything remarkably unattractive in the equivalent physical changes in men. Men are "allowed" to look older without sexual penalty.

Thus, the reason that women experience aging with more pain than men is not simply that they care more than men about how they look. Men also care about their looks and want to be attractive, but since the business of men is mainly being and doing, rather than appearing, the standards for appearance are much less exacting. The standards for what is attractive in a man are permissive; they conform to what is possible or "natural" to most men throughout most of their lives. The standards for women's appearance go against nature, and to come anywhere near approximating them takes considerable effort and time. Women must try to be beautiful. At the least, they are under heavy social pressure not to be ugly. A woman's fortunes depend, far more than a man's, on being at least "acceptable" looking. Men are not subject to this pressure. Good looks in a man is a bonus, not a psychological necessity for maintaining normal self-esteem.

Behind the fact that women are more severely penalized than men are for aging is the fact that people, in this culture at least, are simply less tolerant of ugliness in women than in men. An ugly woman is never merely repulsive. Ugliness in a woman is felt by everyone, men as well as women, to be faintly embarrassing. And many features or blemishes that count as ugly in a woman's face would be quite tolerable on the face of a man. This is not, I would insist, just because the aesthetic standards for men and women are different. It is rather because the aesthetic standards for women are much higher, and narrower, than those proposed for men.

Beauty, women's business in this society, is the theater of their enslavement. Only one standard of female beauty is sanctioned: the *girl*. The great advantage men have is that our culture allows two standards of male beauty: the *boy* and the *man*. The beauty of a boy resembles the beauty of a girl. In both sexes it is a fragile kind of beauty and flourishes naturally only in the early part of the life cycle. Happily, men are able to accept themselves under another standard of good looks—heavier, rougher, more thickly built. A man does not grieve when he loses the smooth, unlined, hairless skin of a boy. For he has only exchanged one form of attractiveness for another: the darker skin of a man's face, roughened by daily shaving, showing the marks of emotion and the normal lines of age. There is no equivalent of this second standard for women. The single standard of beauty for women dictates that they must go on having clear skin. Every wrinkle, every line, every gray hair, is a defeat. No wonder that no boy minds becoming a man, while even the passage from girlhood to early woman-hood is experienced by many women as their downfall, for all women are trained to want to continue looking like girls.

This is not to say there are no beautiful older women. But the standard of beauty in a woman of any age is how far she retains, or how she manages to simulate, the ap-pearance of youth. The exceptional woman in her sixties who is beautiful certainly owes a large debt to her genes. Delayed aging, like good looks, tends to run in families. But nature rarely offers enough to meet this culture's standards. Most of the women who successfully delay the appearance of age are rich, with unlimited leisure to de-vote to nurturing along nature's gifts. Often they are ac-tresses. (That is, highly paid professionals at doing what all women are taught to practice as amateurs.) Such women as Mae West, Dietrich, Stella Adler, Dolores del Río, do not challenge the rule about the relation between beauty and age in women. They are admired precisely because they *are* exceptions, because they have managed (at least so it seems in photographs) to outwit nature. Such miracles,

exceptions made by nature (with the help of art and social privilege), only confirm the rule, because what makes
these women seem beautiful to us is precisely that they
do not look their real age. Society allows no place in our
imagination for a beautiful old woman who does look like
an old woman—a woman who might be like Picasso at the
age of ninety, being photographed outdoors on his estate
in the South of France, wearing only shorts and sandals.
No one imagines such a woman exists. Even the special
exceptions—Mae West & Co.—are always photographed
indoors, cleverly lit, from the most flattering angle and
fully, artfully clothed. The implication is they would not
stand a closer scrutiny. The idea of an old woman in a bath-
ing suit being attractive, or even just acceptable-looking, is
inconceivable. An older woman is, by definition, sexually
repulsive—unless, in fact, she doesn't look old at all. The
body of an old woman, unlike that of an old man, is always
understood as a body that can no longer be shown, offered,
unveiled. At best, it may appear in costume. People still
feel uneasy, thinking about what they might see if her
mask dropped, if she took off her clothes.

Thus, the point for women of dressing up, applying
makeup, dyeing their hair, going on crash diets, and getting face-lifts is not just to be attractive. They are ways
of defending themselves against a profound level of disapproval directed toward women, a disapproval that can
take the form of aversion. The double standard about aging converts the life of women into an inexorable march
toward a condition in which they are not just unattractive,

but disgusting. The profoundest terror of a woman's life is the moment represented in a statue by Rodin called *Old Age* [*The Old Courtesan*]: a naked old woman, seated, pathetically contemplates her flat, pendulous, ruined body. Aging in women is a process of becoming obscene sexually, for the flabby bosom, wrinkled neck, spotted hands, thinning white hair, waistless torso, and veined legs of an old woman are felt to be obscene. In our direst moments of the imagination, this transformation can take place with dismaying speed—as in the end of *Lost Horizon*, when the beautiful young girl is carried by her lover out of Shangri-La and, within minutes, turns into a withered, repulsive crone. There is no equivalent nightmare about men. This is why, however much a man may care about his appearance, that caring can never acquire the same desperateness it often does for women. When men dress according to fashion or now even use cosmetics, they do not expect from clothes and makeup what women do. A face-lotion or perfume or deodorant or hair spray, used by a man, is not part of a disguise. Men, as men, do not feel the need to disguise themselves to fend off morally disapproved signs of aging, to outwit premature sexual obsolescence, to cover up aging as obscenity. Men are not subject to the barely concealed revulsion expressed in this culture against the female body—except in its smooth, youthful, firm, odorless, blemish-free form.

One of the attitudes that punish women most severely is the visceral horror felt at aging female flesh. It reveals a radical fear of women installed deep in this culture, a demonology of women that has crystallized in such mythic caricatures as the vixen, the virago, the vamp, and the witch. Several centuries of witch-phobia, during which one of the cruelest extermination programs in Western history was carried out, suggest something of the extremity of this fear. That old women are repulsive is one of the most profound aesthetic and erotic feelings in our culture. Women share it as much as men do. (Oppressors, as a rule, deny oppressed people their own "native" standards of beauty. And the oppressed end up being convinced that they *are* ugly.) How women are psychologically damaged by this misogynistic idea of what is beautiful parallels the way in which Blacks have been deformed in a society that has up to now defined beautiful as white. Psychological tests made on young Black children in the United States some years ago showed how early and how thoroughly they incorporate the white standard of good looks. Virtually all the children expressed fantasies that indicated they considered Black people to be ugly, funny-looking, dirty, brutish. A similar kind of self-hatred infects most women. Like men, they find old age in women "uglier" than old age in men.

This aesthetic taboo functions, in sexual attitudes, as a racial taboo. In this society most people feel an involuntary recoil of the flesh when imagining a middle-aged woman making love with a young man—exactly as many whites flinch viscerally at the thought of a white woman in bed with a Black man. The banal drama of a man of fifty who leaves a wife of forty-five for a girlfriend of twenty-eight contains no strictly sexual outrage, whatever sympathy people may have for the abandoned wife. On the contrary. Everyone "understands." Everyone knows that men like girls, that young women often want middle-aged men. But no one "understands" the reverse situation. A woman of forty-five who leaves a husband of fifty for a lover of twenty-eight is the makings of a social and sexual scandal at a deep level of feeling. No one takes exception to a romantic couple in which the man is twenty years or more the woman's senior. The movies pair Joanne Dru and John Wayne, Marilyn Monroe and Joseph Cotten, Audrey Hepburn and Cary Grant, Jane Fonda and Yves Montand, Catherine Deneuve and Marcello Mastroianni; as in actual life, these are perfectly plausible, appealing couples. When the age difference runs the other way, people are puzzled and embarrassed and simply shocked. (Remember Joan Crawford and Cliff Robertson in *Autumn Leaves*? But so troubling is this kind of love story that it rarely figures in the movies, and then only as the melancholy history of a failure.) The usual view of why a woman of forty and a boy of twenty, or a woman of fifty and a man of thirty, marry is that the man is seeking a mother, not a wife; no one believes the marriage will last. For a woman to respond erotically and romantically to a man who, in terms of his age, could be her father is considered normal. A man who falls in love with a woman who, however attractive she may be, is old enough to be his mother is thought to be extremely neurotic (victim of an "Oedipal fixation" is the fashionable tag), if not mildly contemptible.

The wider the gap in age between partners in a couple, the more obvious is the prejudice against women. When old men, such as Justice Douglas, Picasso, Strom Thurmond, Onassis, Chaplin, and Pablo Casals, take brides thirty, forty, fifty years younger than themselves, it strikes people as remarkable, perhaps an exaggeration—but still plausible. To explain such a match, people enviously attribute some special virility and charm to the man. Though he can't be handsome, he is famous; and his fame is understood as having boosted his attractiveness to women. People imagine that his young wife, respectful of her elderly husband's attainments, is happy to become his helper. For the man a late marriage is always good public relations. It adds to the impression that, despite his advanced age, he is still to be reckoned with; it is the sign of a continuing vitality presumed to be available as well to his art, business activity, or political career. But an elderly woman who married a young man would be greeted quite differently. She would have broken a fierce taboo, and she would get no credit for her courage. Far from being admired for her vitality, she would probably be condemned as predatory, willful, selfish, exhibitionistic. At the same time she would be pitied, since such a marriage would be taken as evidence that she was in her dotage. If she had a conventional career or were in business or held public office, she would quickly suffer from the current of disapproval. Her very credibility as a professional would decline, since people would suspect that her young husband might have an undue influence on her. Her "respectability" would certainly be compromised. Indeed, the well-known old women I can think of who dared such unions, if only at the end of their lives—George Eliot, Colette, Édith Piaf—have all belonged to that category of people, creative artists and entertainers, who have special license from society to behave scandalously. It is thought to be a scandal for a woman to ignore that she is old and therefore too ugly for a young man. Her looks and a certain physical condition determine a woman's desirability, not her talents or her needs. Women are not supposed to be "potent." A marriage between an old woman and a young man subverts the very ground rule of relations between the two sexes, that is: whatever the variety of appearances, men remain dominant. Their claims come first. Women are supposed to be the associates and companions of men, not their full equals—and never their superiors. Women are to remain in the state of a permanent "minority."

The convention that wives should be younger than their husbands powerfully enforces the "minority" status of women, since being senior in age always carries with it, in any relationship, a certain amount of power and authority. There are no laws on the matter, of course. The convention is obeyed because to do otherwise makes one feel as if one is doing something ugly or in bad taste. Everyone feels intuitively the aesthetic rightness of a marriage in which the man is older than the woman, which means that any marriage in which the woman is older creates a dubious or less gratifying mental picture. Everyone is addicted to the visual pleasure that women give by meeting certain aesthetic requirements from which men are exempted, which keeps women working at staying youthful-looking while men are left free to age. On a deeper level everyone finds the signs of old age in women aesthetically offensive, which conditions one to feel automatically repelled by the prospect of an elderly woman marrying a much younger man. The situation in which women are kept minors for life is largely organized by such conformist, unreflective preferences. But taste is not free, and its judgments are never merely "natural." Rules of taste enforce structures of power. The revulsion against aging in women is the cutting edge of a whole set of oppressive structures (often masked as gallantries) that keep women in their place.

The ideal state proposed for women is docility, which means not being fully grown up. Most of what is cherished as typically "feminine" is simply behavior that is childish, immature, weak. To offer so low and demeaning a standard of fulfillment in itself constitutes oppression in an acute form—a sort of moral neocolonialism. But women are not simply condescended to by the values that secure the dominance of men. They are repudiated. Perhaps because of having been their oppressors for so long, few men really *like* women (though they love individual women), and few men ever feel really comfortable or at ease in women's company. This malaise arises because relations between the two sexes are rife with hypocrisy, as men manage to love those they dominate and therefore don't respect. Oppressors always try to justify their privileges and brutalities by imagining that those they oppress belong to a lower order of civilization or are less than fully "human." Deprived of part of their ordinary human dignity, the oppressed take on certain "demonic" traits. The oppressions of large groups have to be anchored deep in the psyche, continually renewed by partly unconscious fears and taboos, by a sense of the obscene. Thus, women arouse not only desire and affection in men but aversion as well. Women are thoroughly domesticated familiars. But, at certain times and in certain situations, they become alien, untouchable. The aversion men feel, so much of which is covered over, is felt most frankly, with least inhibition, toward the type of woman who is most taboo "aesthetically," a woman who has become—with the natural changes brought about by aging—obscene.

Nothing more clearly demonstrates the vulnerability of women than the special pain, confusion, and bad faith with which they experience getting older. And in the struggle that some women are waging on behalf of all women to be treated (and treat themselves) as full human beings—not "only" as women—one of the earliest results to be hoped for is that women become aware, indignantly aware, of the double standard about aging from which they suffer so harshly.

It is understandable that women often succumb to the

temptation to lie about their age. Given society's double standard, to question a woman about her age is indeed often an aggressive act, a trap. Lying is an elementary means of self-defense, a way of scrambling out of the trap, at least temporarily. To expect a woman, after "a certain age," to tell exactly how old she is—when she has a chance, either through the generosity of nature or the cleverness of art, to pass for being somewhat younger than she actually is—is like expecting a landowner to admit that the estate he has put up for sale is actually worth less than the buyer is prepared to pay. The double standard about aging sets women up as property, as objects whose value depreciates rapidly with the march of the calendar.

The prejudices that mount against women as they grow older are an important arm of male privilege. It is the present unequal distribution of adult roles between the two sexes that gives men a freedom to age denied to women. Men actively administer the double standard about aging because the "masculine" role awards them the initiative in courtship. Men choose; women are chosen. So men choose younger women. But although this system of inequality is operated by men, it could not work if women themselves did not acquiesce in it. Women reinforce it powerfully with their complacency, with their anguish, with their lies.

Not only do women lie more than men do about their age but men forgive them for it, thereby confirming their own superiority. A man who lies about his age is thought to be weak, "unmanly." A woman who lies about her age is behaving in a quite acceptable, "feminine" way. Petty lying is viewed by men with indulgence, one of a number of patronizing allowances made for women. It has the same moral unimportance as the fact that women are often late for appointments. Women are not expected to be truthful, or punctual, or expert in handling and repairing machines, or frugal, or physically brave. They are expected to be second-class adults, whose natural state is that of a grateful dependence on men. And so they often are, since that is what they are brought up to be. So far as women heed the stereotypes of "feminine" behavior, they *cannot* behave as fully responsible, independent adults.

Most women share the contempt for women expressed in the double standard about aging—to such a degree that they take their lack of self-respect for granted. Women have been accustomed so long to the protection of their masks, their smiles, their endearing lies. Without this protection, they know, they would be more vulnerable. But in protecting themselves as women, they betray themselves as adults. The model corruption in a woman's life is denying her age. She symbolically accedes to all those myths that furnish women with their imprisoning securities and privileges, that create their genuine oppression, that inspire their real discontent. Each time a woman lies about her age she becomes an accomplice in her own underdevelopment as a human being.

Women have another option. They can aspire to be wise, not merely nice; to be competent, not merely helpful; to be strong, not merely graceful; to be ambitious for themselves, not merely for themselves in relation to men and children. They can let themselves age naturally and without embarrassment, actively protesting and disobeying the conventions that stem from this society's double standard about aging. Instead of being girls, girls as long as possible, who then age humiliatingly into middle-aged women and then obscenely into old women, they can become women much earlier—and remain active adults, enjoying the long, erotic career of which women are capable, far longer. Women should allow their faces to show the lives they have lived. Women should tell the truth.

(1972)

The Third World of Women

Author's Note: The following text was written in July 1972 in re-sponse to a questionnaire sent to me and five other women (includ-ing Simone de Beauvoir and the Italian communist deputy Rossana Rossanda) by the editors of Libre, *a new Spanish-language politi-cal and literary quarterly with a loosely Marxist orientation, edited in Paris. It was published in the October 1972 issue of* Libre, *no. 3, in a translation by the Spanish novelist Juan Goytisolo. Most of the readers of* Libre *live in Latin America, which explains the painstak-ingly explicit character of what I wrote. The nature of the magazine's readership explains as well my freedom to assume, when writing my answers, that a revolutionary socialist view of the subject is, at the very least, something to contend with. In the United States, where militant feminism is a livelier and much more widely heard point of view right now than it is anywhere else, discussion tends to be less and less explicit about the root questions, and rarely even alludes to the Marxist analysis. Nevertheless, because the formula-tion of a political perspective is still everywhere in its early stages, that seems to me to justify printing here what I wrote for a quite different audience.*

A few paragraphs first, a sort of prologue, a response to a more general question which you don't ask: *At what stage now is the struggle for women's liberation?*

For thousands of years, practically everyone in the world assumed that it lay in the "nature" of the human species that some people were superior (and should be masters) and other people were inferior (and should be slaves). Only about 150 years ago did elements of the ruling classes begin to suspect that slavery was not really, after all, "natural," and that the undeniably servile and culturally underdeveloped character of slaves could be explained by the very fact that these people were slaves, were brought up to be slaves—instead of proving that they deserved to be slaves.

Support for the emancipation of women stands today approximately where support for the emancipation of slaves stood two centuries ago. Just as throughout the millennia of unquestioning acceptance of slavery, the age-old oppression of women is justified by an appeal to presumed inequalities "natural" to the species, the vast majority of people on this planet—women as well as men—remain convinced that women have a different "nature" than men, and that these "natural" differences make women inferior.

Educated people in urbanized countries, especially those who regard themselves as liberals or socialists, often deny they believe these differences make women inferior. That women differ from men, they argue, does not mean that women are not the equal of men. Their argument is as dishonest as the separate-but-equal argument once used to defend the legal segregation of the races in schools. For the specific content of these supposedly innate differences between women and men imply a scale of values in which the qualities assigned to women are clearly less estimable than those assigned to men. "Masculinity" is identified with competence, autonomy, self-control, ambition, risk-taking, independence, rationality; "femininity" is identified with incompetence, helplessness, irrationality, passivity, noncompetitiveness, being nice. Women are trained for second-class adulthood, most of what is cherished as typically "feminine" behavior being simply behavior that is childish, servile, weak, immature. No wonder men balk at accepting women as their full equals. *Vive la différence* indeed!

Not expecting women to be truthful, or punctual, or expert in handling and repairing machines, or frugal, or muscular, or physically brave makes all women who are—exceptional. Every generation produces a few women of genius (or at least of irrepressible eccentricity) who win special status for themselves. But the historical visibility of the Trung sisters, Joan of Arc, Saint Teresa, Mademoiselle Maupin, George Eliot, Louise Michel, Harriet Tubman, Isabelle Eberhardt, Marie Curie, Rosa Luxemburg, Amelia Earhart, and the other of that small band is understood to follow precisely from their possessing qualities that women do not normally have. Such women are credited with "masculine" energy, intelligence, willfulness, and courage. Examples of unusually capable and genuinely independent women do not shake the general presumption of women's inferiority, any more than the discovery (and favored treatment) of intellectually talented slaves made cultivated Roman slaveowners doubt the naturalness of slavery: the argument from "nature" is self-confirming. Individual lives which do not confirm the argument will always be taken as exceptions, thereby leaving the stereotypes intact.

Historically, or rather prehistorically, the oppression of women must have arisen out of certain practical arrangements to insure their special biological responsibility: childbearing. The elaborate forms of women's oppression—psychological, political, economic, cultural—all refer back to the biological division of labor. But the fact that women bear children while men do not hardly proves that women and men are fundamentally different. It rather indicates how slim is the basis in "nature" for the supposed difference—whereby women's reproductive physiology is converted into a life-vocation, with its appropriately narrow norms of character and temperament. But even physiological "nature" is not an immutable fact with unchanging consequences. It, too, is part of history—and evolves with history. If the whole difference between women and men ultimately rests on the fact that women are busy bearing children, then the circumstances in which that vocation is exercised have been severely modified: if "nature" has supplied the pretext for women's enslavement, then history now supplies the objective conditions for their social and psychological liberation. For it is just this importance of the physiological difference between women and men which is becoming obsolete.

The Industrial Revolution provided the material base for a reconsideration of slavery; when machines were invented that were more productive and efficient than unpaid labor, it became reasonable to free people from legal bondage to work. Now the Ecological Turning Point (increased longevity, plus the population explosion, plus the rapid depletion of natural resources) makes it not only possible but ultimately imperative that most women be freed from all but the most minimal relation to their biological responsibility. Once the reproductive destiny of women shrinks to two, one, or no pregnancies (with every likelihood that, for the first time in history, almost all children born will live to adulthood), the underlying rationale for the repressive definition of women as servile, domestic, primarily childrearing creatures collapses. As the Industrial Revolution encouraged people to rethink the "naturalness" of slavery, so the new ecological era which the planet entered in the middle of the twentieth century is enabling people to rethink the hitherto self-evident "femininity" of women. The "femininity" of women and the "masculinity" of men are morally defective and historically obsolete conceptions. The liberation of women seems to me as much a historical necessity as the abolition of slavery—like abolition, a hopeless-looking cause before it actually triumphs; even more momentous than abolition in its psychic and historical consequences.

But, anachronistic as their oppression may be, women

will not be liberated without a hard struggle, a struggle that really does deserve the adjective "revolutionary." This revolution must be both radical and conservative. It is conservative in the sense that it will reject the ideology of unlimited growth (ever-increasing levels of productivity and consumption; the unlimited cannibalization of the environment)—an ideology shared with equal enthusiasm by the countries which call themselves capitalist and by those which aspire to communism. It is radical in the sense that it will challenge, and remake, the basically authoritarian moral habits common to both capitalist and communist countries. Liberating women is the most radical part of this new revolutionary process.

In opposition to the whole accredited modern tradition about revolution, I am arguing that what used to be called "the woman question" not only exists but exists independently of the issues generally posed by political radicals. Marx, Engels, Lenin, Trotsky, Luxemburg, and Gramsci held that the oppression of women was not a separate problem, but rather one to be absorbed by the class struggle and eventually resolved by the creation of socialism. I do not agree. The fact is, no government which claims to operate on part of Marx's legacy has rethought the condition of women. On the contrary, every communist country has been content with offering women merely liberal improvements in their situations—like increased access to education and jobs and divorces—while preserving intact the overwhelming monopoly of political power by men, and leaving unchanged the structures of repression that characterize private relations between the two sexes. But this striking failure of all countries where left-revolutionary governments have come to power to do anything "radical" for women should not be surprising. In none of the many edifying declarations made by the principal theorists of proletarian revolution in favor of emancipating women has the true complexity of the question ever been grasped. Marxists have not properly estimated the depth of sexism any more than, in setting out to defeat imperialism, they properly estimated the depths of racism.

Now, to the questions you do ask.

1. What meaning does the idea of women's liberation have for you?

One often hears now that the liberation of women cannot take place without the liberation of men. The cliché is true, up to a point. Women and men share the same ultimate aim: to gain genuine autonomy, which means participating in (and being let alone by) a society that is not based on alienation and repression. But the cliché is also dangerous, for it implicitly denies that there are stages in the struggle to liberate women. Like many clichés which are true, it disarms thought and pacifies rage. It encourages a passive and merely reformist view of the problem. (Thus, aptly enough, "the liberation of women equals the liberation of men" is the official slogan of the Swedish government's eminently superficial policies for securing equality for women within the framework of sophisticated liberal capitalism.)

To be sure, every human being in this imperfect world stands in need of liberation—masters as well as slaves, oppressors as well as the oppressed. But a just society cannot be accurately conceived, or fought for, in a unitary or universal way. Liberating a Thai peasant is not the same as liberating a white factory worker in Detroit. The oppression of women does not, in terms of fundamental structures, resemble the oppression of men.

Reasonable-sounding as the idea may be, it is simply not true that the liberation of men and the liberation of women are two parts of a reciprocal process. However much men too are deformed psychologically by sexist stereotypes, these stereotypes do confer undeniable privileges on them. Men have a greater range of behavior available to them than women have, and they have considerably more mobility in the world. (Simply consider the fact that in *most* places she might go in "the world," a woman alone risks rape or physical violence. Basically, a woman is only safe at "home" or when protected by a man.) In the most concrete way, in that he need not always be on guard against predatory assault, a man is always better off than a woman. Men (and women) are oppressed by other men. But all women are oppressed by all men.

The cliché that when women are liberated men will be liberated too shamelessly slides over the raw reality of male domination—as if this were an arrangement in fact arranged by nobody, which suits nobody, which works to nobody's advantage. In fact, the very opposite is true. The domination of men over women is to the advantage of men; the liberation of women will be at the expense of male privilege. Perhaps afterward, in some happy sense, men will be liberated too—liberated from the tiresome obligation to be "masculine." But allowing oppressors to lay down their psychological burdens is quite another, secondary sense of liberation. The first priority is to liberate the oppressed. Never before in history have the claims of oppressed and oppressors turned out to be, on inspection, quite harmonious. It will not be true this time either.

All women live in an "imperialist" situation in which men are colonialists and women are natives. In so-called Third World countries, the situation of women with respect to men is tyrannically, brutally colonialist. In economically advanced countries (both capitalist and communist) the situation of women is neocolonialist: the segregation of women has been liberalized; the use of physical force against women has declined; men delegate some of their authority, their rule is less overtly institutionalized. But the same basic relations of inferiority and superiority, of powerlessness and power, of cultural underdevelopment and cultural privilege, prevail between women and men in all countries.

Any serious program for liberating women must start from the premise that liberation is not just about *equality* (the "liberal" idea). It is about *power*. Women cannot be liberated without reducing the power of men. Their liberation not only means changing consciousness and social

49

structures in ways that will transfer to women much of the power monopolized by men. The nature of power itself will thereby change, since throughout history power has itself been defined in sexist terms—being identified with normative, supposedly innate masculine taste for aggressiveness and physical coercion, and with the ceremonies and prerogatives of all-male groupings in war, government, religion, sport, and commerce. Anything less than a change in who has power and what power is, is not liberation but pacification. Changes that are not profound buy off the resentment that threatens established authority. Ameliorating an unstable and too oppressive rule—as when old empires replace colonialist by neocolonialist forms of exploitation—actually serves to regenerate the existing forms of dominance.

To advocate that women make a common front with men to bring about their mutual liberation pulls a veil over the harsh realities of the power relations that determine all dialogue between the sexes. It is not for women to assume the task of liberating men, when they have first to liberate themselves—which means exploring the grounds of enmity, unsweetened for the moment by the dream of reconciliation. Women must change themselves; they must change one another, without worrying about how this will affect men. The consciousness of women will change only when they think about themselves, and forget about what is good for their men. Supposing that these changes can be undertaken in collaboration with men minimizes (and trivializes) the range and depths of women's struggle.

If women change, men will be forced to change. But these changes in men will not occur without considerable resistance. No ruling class ever ceded its real privileges without a struggle. The very structure of society is founded on male privilege, and men will not cede their privileges simply because doing so is more humane or just. Men may make concessions, reluctantly granting women more "civil rights." In most countries now, women can vote and attend institutions of higher education and are permitted to train for the professions. Within the next twenty years, they will get equal pay for equal work and be granted effective ownership of their own bodies (through easy access to contraceptives and the legalization of abortion). But these concessions, however desirable they may be, do not challenge the fundamental attitudes that maintain women as second-class citizens nor touch the root of male privileges.

A radical, as opposed to a liberal, change in the status of women will abolish the mystique of "nature." Women should work toward an end to *all* stereotyping of any kind, positive as well as negative, according to people's sexual identity. Changing the laws that discriminate against women in specific situations (with respect to suffrage, entering into contracts, access to education, and employment) is not enough. The forms of work, sexual customs, the idea of family life have to be altered; language itself, which crudely enshrines the ancient bias against women, cannot remain unaffected. For, however advanced our ideas, every time we speak we continue to affirm the superiority (activity) of men and the inferiority (passivity) of women. It is "grammatically correct" to assume that agents, active persons are men. Grammar, the ultimate arena of sexist brainwashing, conceals the very existence of women—except in special situations. Thus we *must* say "he" when we mean a person who might be of either sex. "Man" is the accepted way to refer to all human beings; "men" is the literary way of saying people. (As "men in dark times," a line from a poem by Brecht and the title of one of Hannah Arendt's books, means people in dark times. Indeed, of the ten people Arendt writes about in her brilliant, noble book two are women. But one, Isak Dinesen, adopted a male pseudonym and the other, Rosa Luxemburg, was, as the jacket copy comments coyly, "the manliest of them all!") The pronoun that substitutes for nouns like student, worker, citizen, artist, public official, athlete, industrialist is "he." Language is not, of course, the source of the prejudice that identifies "men" as the human race, and associates most human activities with men only. Language merely expresses the sexist order that has prevailed throughout history.

The women's movement has already made the sexist bias of grammar feel offensive to a vocal minority of women. Sensitizing increasing numbers of people to sexism in language—as most people have only recently become alert to racist clichés in language (and art)—is an important task. More generally, people must be helped to wake up to the profound misogyny expressed on all levels of human interchange, not just in laws but in the detail of everyday life: in forms of politeness and in the conventions (clothes, gestures, etc.) which polarize sexual identity, and in the flow of images (in art, news, and advertising) which perpetuate sexist stereotypes. These attitudes will change only when women free themselves from their "nature" and start creating and inhabiting another history.

2. In the process of liberating women, do you give equal importance to economic liberation and to sexual liberation?

The question seems to me to reveal the underlying weakness of the very concept of "liberation." Unless made more specific, "women's liberation" is an empty goal—and one which blurs the focus and dilutes the energy of women's struggle. I am not sure that the economic and the sexual are two different kinds of liberation. But suppose that they are or, at least, that they can be considered separately. Without more clarity about what women are being liberated from and for, it is meaningless to ask whether both liberations are equally important.

The notion of "economic liberation" can be used to cover up the real issues. That women have access to a wide variety of jobs outside the home for which they are properly paid is certainly a primary, unnegotiable demand. The key to women's psychological and cultural underdevelopment is the fact that most women do not support themselves—neither in the literal (economic) nor metaphoric (psychological, cultural) sense. But it is hardly enough for women to secure the *possibility* of earning money through the opening up of more jobs, through the creation of free facilities for the care of young children. Work must not be merely an option, an alternative to the still more common (and normative) "career" of housewife and mother. It must be *expected* that most women will work, that they will be economically independent (whether married or not) just as men are. Without work, women will never break the chains of dependence on men—the minimal prerequisite for their becoming fully adult. Unless they work, and their work is usually as valuable as their husbands', married women have not even the chance of gaining real power over their own lives, which means the power to change their lives. The arts of psychological coercion and conciliation for which women are notorious—flattery, charm, wheedling, glamour, tears—are a servile substitute for real influence and autonomy.

Simply being able to work, however, hardly means that a woman is "liberated." Large numbers of women already do work, and of these a minority already earns wages that guarantee economic independence; yet most women who work remain as dependent as ever on men. The reason is that employment itself is organized along sexist lines. The colonialized status of women is confirmed and indeed strengthened by the sexist division of labor. Women do not participate gainfully in modern work on the same footing as men. They play a supportive, backup role in the economy. What they do in "the world" tends to reproduce their image as "household" (serving and nurturing) creatures;

they are considered unfit for large executive responsibilities. Thus, women cannot be said to be economically liberated until they perform *all* activities now performed by men, on the same terms (with respect to wages, standards of performance, exposure to risk) as men—thereby relinquishing the prerogatives of the fool, the child, and the servant. Their economic liberation is essential not merely to the psychological and moral well-being of individual women. Until they become important to the economy, not just as a reserve labor pool but because in large numbers they possess the major professional and executive skills, women have no means of exercising political power, which means gaining control of institutions and having an effective say in how society will change in the coming decades. Once again: liberation means *power*—or it hardly means anything at all.

The notion of "sexual liberation" seems to me even more suspect. The ancient double standard, which imputes to women less sexual energy and fewer sexual desires than men (and punishes them for behavior condoned in men), is clearly a way of keeping women in their place. But to demand for women the same privileges of sexual experimentation that men have is not enough, since the very conception of sexuality is an instrument of repression. Most sexual relationships act out the attitudes which oppress women and perpetuate male privilege. Merely to remove the onus placed on the sexual expressiveness of women is a hollow victory if the sexuality they become freer to enjoy remains the old one that converts women into objects. The mores of late, urban capitalist society have been for some time, as everyone has noticed, increasingly more "permissive," penalizing women much less than before for behaving like sexual beings outside the context of monogamous marriage. But this already "freer" sexuality mostly reflects a spurious idea of freedom: the right of each person, briefly, to exploit and dehumanize someone else.

Without a change in the very norms of sexuality, the liberation of women is a meaningless goal. Sex as such is not liberating for women. Neither is more sex.

The question is: *What* sexuality are women to be liberated to enjoy? The only sexual ethic liberating for women is one which challenges the primacy of genital heterosexuality. A nonrepressive society, a society in which women are subjectively and objectively the genuine equals of men, will necessarily be an androgynous society. Why? Because the only other plausible terms on which the oppression of women could be ended are that men and women decide to live apart, and that is impossible. Separatism does remain plausible as a way of putting an end to the oppression of "colored" peoples by the white race. Conceivably, the different races originating in different parts of the planet could agree to live quite separately again (with the habits and mentalities of each strictly protected against all incursions of cultural as well as economic imperialism). But women and men will undoubtedly always cohabit. If, therefore, the answer to sexism—unlike racism—is not even conceivably separatism, then defending the distinct moral and aesthetic "traditions" of each sex (to preserve something equivalent to "cultural plurality") and attacking the single standard of intellectual excellence or rationality as male "cultural imperialism" (to revalidate the unknown and despised "women's culture") are misleading tactics in the struggle to liberate women.

The aim of struggle should not be to protect the differences between the two sexes but to undermine them. To create a nonrepressive relation between women and men means to erase as far as possible the conventional demarcation lines that have been set up between the two sexes, to reduce the tension between women and men that arises from "otherness." As everyone has noticed, there has been a lively tendency among young people in recent years to narrow and even confuse sex differences in clothes, hairstyles, gestures, taste. But this first step toward depolarizing the sexes, partly co-opted within capitalist forms of consumership as mere "style" (the commerce of unisex boutiques), will be denied its political implications unless the tendency takes root at a deeper level.

The more profound depolarization of the sexes must take place in the world of work and, increasingly, in sexual relations themselves. As "otherness" is reduced, some of the energy of sexual attraction between the sexes will decline. Women and men will certainly continue to make love and to pair off in couples. But women and men will no longer *primarily* define each other as potential sexual partners. In a nonrepressive nonsexist society, sexuality will in one sense have a more important role than it has today—because it will be more diffused. Homosexual choices will be as valid and respectable as heterosexual choices; both will grow out of a genuine bisexuality. (Exclusive homosexuality—which, like exclusive heterosexuality, is learned—would be much less common in a nonsexist society than it is at present.) But in such a society, sexuality will in another sense be less important than it is now—because sexual relations will no longer be hysterically craved as a substitute for genuine freedom and for so many other pleasures (intimacy, intensity, feeling of belonging, blasphemy) which this society frustrates.

3. In your opinion, what is the relationship between the struggle for women's liberation and the class struggle? Do you believe the first must be subordinated to the second?

I see little relation at present between the class struggle and the struggle to liberate women. The double content of modern left-revolutionary politics—the overthrow of one class by another within a nation, and the freeing of colonialized peoples from imperialist control—is basically irrelevant to the struggle of women as women. Women are neither a class nor a nation. Politically radical women may well prefer to participate in existing insurgent movements than to limit their energies, as they see it, to the struggle of women. But in doing so they should realize that, at the most, all that such multi-issue revolutionary politics (like parliamentary party politics) offers women is reformist gains, the promise of formal "equality."

Which level of struggle should come first? I don't see how one can take a general position about that. The priorities of struggle vary from nation to nation, from historical moment to historical moment—and depend, within a given nation, on one's race and one's social class. It seems beyond question that the liberation of women in Vietnam has to be subordinated at the present time to the struggle for national liberation. In the affluent countries, however, the liberation of women is a much more immediately relevant issue—both in itself and for its usefulness in radicalizing people for other forms of struggle. (For instance, to explore the nature of women's oppression helps one to understand the nature of imperialism. And the other way around.)

As I see it, the main point about the relationship of the struggle of women to what Marxist-oriented revolutionary movements define as the central struggle, the class struggle, is the following. To liberate women requires a cultural revolution that will attack attitudes and mental habits which otherwise could well survive the reconstruction of economic relationships that is the goal of the class struggle. The position of women could, conceivably, be scarcely affected by a change in class relationships. Because Marx and Engels were humanists, heirs of the Enlightenment, they denounced the oppression of women under capitalism. But the traditional "feminism" of Marx and his successors is not *logically* connected with the Marxist analysis. (Neither, I would argue, is Freud's coarse "antifeminism" *logically* connected with the basic ideas of psychoanalytic theory.)

Socialism will not inevitably bring about the liberation of women. Nevertheless, only in a society that one calls, for want of a better name, socialist would it be *possible* to invent and institutionalize forms of life that would liberate women. Therefore, though the struggle to build socialism and the cause of women's liberation are hardly identical, militant feminists do have a vested interest in the fortunes of a revolutionary socialist movement and good reason to be, if only tacitly, allies—as they have reason to be the enemies of all right-revolutionary (or fascist) movements, which always preach the reinforcement of male privilege and the subservience of women.

4. Do you think the fact that the work of a housewife is unsalaried and has no exchange value on the labor market makes women a separate class existing apart from other economic classes? Do you view patriarchal oppression as a principal or secondary contradiction in modern society?

No. The fact that "housework," which is defined as women's work, is physical and, unlike work done in the "world," unpaid does not put women into a separate economic class. Women do not form a class any more than men do. Like men, women make up half the membership of every class. The wives, sisters, and daughters of rich men participate in the oppression of the poor; by virtue of their class membership rather than their sex, a minority of women oppress other women. If a label is needed, women could perhaps be considered a caste. But this is only an analogy. There is no suitable label to be borrowed from other vocabularies of social analysis. To suppose that women constitute a class makes no more sense than to suppose that Blacks are a class. The human species is divided into two sexes (and "caste"-type relations based on sexual identity), as well as a plurality of races (with "caste"-type relations based mainly on color). The oppression of one class by another is only one form of oppression. The structures built around the existence of two sexes, like those built around the existence of many races, are irreducible to structures built around the existence of social classes—although, obviously, oppressions can and often do overlap.

I detect in this question a pious hope that the oppression of women could be blamed on a particular form of society, a particular set of class arrangements. But it can't. If socialism—at least as it exists so far—is not self-evidently the solution, neither is capitalism self-evidently the culprit. Women have always been treated as inferior, have always been marginal politically and culturally. The oppression of women constitutes the most fundamental type of repression in organized societies. That is, it is the most *ancient* form of oppression, predating all oppression based on class, caste, and race. It is the most primitive form of hierarchy.

Because this is so I do not see how "patriarchal oppression" (your term) can be considered as any kind of contradiction, either principal or secondary. On the contrary, the structure of this society is precisely based on patriarchal oppression, the undoing of which will modify the most deeply rooted habits of friendship and love, the conceptions of work, the ability to wage war (which is profoundly nourished by sexist anxieties), and the mechanisms of power. The very nature of power in organized societies is founded on sexist models of conduct. Power is defined in terms of, and feeds on, machismo.

Modern industrial society certainly contains many contradictory structures and ideologies, but the struggle to liberate women cannot be expected to succeed, in my opinion, if it is mainly directed toward trying to aggravate and intensify already existing contradictions; the task is not so much to exploit a contradiction as to dislodge this most profoundly rooted of structures. The women's movement must lead to a critical assault on the very nature of the state—the millennial tyranny of patriarchal rule being the low-keyed model of the peculiarly modern tyranny of the fascist state.

I would maintain that fascism, far from being a political aberration whose greatest plausibility was confined to Europe and the interval between the two World Wars, is the *normal* condition of the modern state: the condition to which the governments of all industrially advanced countries tend. Fascism, in other words, is the natural development of the values of the patriarchal state applied to the conditions (and contradictions) of twentieth-century "mass" societies. Virginia Woolf was altogether correct when she declared in the late 1930s, in a remarkable tract called *Three Guineas*, that the fight to liberate women is a fight against fascism.

5. It is often said that most salaried work in present-day society is alienating. In spite of this, do you advise women to seek salaried employment as a means of liberation?

However alienating most salaried work may be, for women it is still liberating to have a job, if only because it frees them from the confinement of domesticity and parasitism. But the commitment to work is only a first step, of course. Women will never be autonomous unless they participate in society's work on terms of complete equality. Women must break out of the ghettos of work in which they are isolated: jobs that continue to exploit their life-long training to be servile, to be both supportive and parasitical, to be unadventurous. For a woman to leave "home" to go out into "the world" and work rarely carries a full commitment to "the world," that is, achievement; in most cases, it is strictly understood to be just a way of earning money, of supplementing the family income. Women fill very few corporate or political posts, and contribute only a tiny contingent to the liberal professions (apart from teaching). Except in communist countries, they are virtually barred from jobs that involve an expert, intimate relation to machines or an aggressive use of the body, or that carry any physical danger or sense of adventure, or that directly compete with (instead of support) what men do. Besides being less well paid, most employment available to women has a low ceiling of advancement and gives meager outlet to normal wishes to be active and to make decisions. The result of these prejudices is that virtually all outstanding work by women in capitalist countries has been voluntary, for few women can stand up to the disapproval unleashed when they deviate from the stereotypes of "feminine" submissiveness and illogicality. (Thus, it is disparaging to describe a woman as "ambitious" or "tough" or "intellectual"; and she will be called "castrating" for behavior that would be viewed, in a man, as normal or even commendable aggressiveness.)

Granted that almost all jobs available in modern societies could be described as alienating, I am more impressed by the double alienation from which women suffer—by being denied even those limited satisfactions that men can derive from work. By entering the world of work in its present forms, women have much to gain. They acquire skills, by which they can take care of themselves and organize themselves better. And they acquire a specific arena of struggle, in each job or profession, where they can press the demands for their liberation.

These demands must go beyond "equality" as that may be achieved between individuals in the work situations to which women are admitted. Far more important than getting the same pay for the same work (though that minimal "liberal" demand has not yet been met in *any* country in the world, including China) is breaking down the sex-stereotyping according to which the world of work is organized. Women must become surgeons, agronomists, lawyers, mechanics, soldiers, electricians, astronauts, factory executives, orchestra conductors, sound engineers, chess players, construction workers, pilots—and in numbers large enough so that their presence is no longer remarked. (When women become the vast majority doing a job formerly monopolized by men, as in the medical profession in the Soviet Union, the challenge to sex-stereotyping is much slighter. The result is that the hitherto "masculine" role of doctor has become a "feminine" role.)

As long as the system of sex segregation in work remains strong, most people—women as well as men—will continue to rationalize it by insisting that women lack the physical strength or the capacity for rational judgment or the emotional self-control to do many jobs. As that system weakens, women will get more competent. And when they are not merely tolerated in but *expected* to perform the jobs from which they are now barred, large numbers of women will in fact be able to do them.

When work becomes fully desegregated sexually, women will be better qualified to join with their coworkers who are men in questioning its fundamental terms, as presently defined. The bureaucratic style in which work in modern society is laid out must be redesigned to provide more democratic, decentralized ways of planning and making decisions. Most important of all, the very ideal of "productivity" (and consumership) must be challenged. The economy of affluent countries operates by a division of function that runs along sexual lines: men are defined as "producers" and tool-users, while women (and adolescents) are defined principally as "consumers." Unless this distinction is subverted, the full admission of women to the work men do will just double the ranks of that great army of psychologically alienated "producers" already drafted into the ecologically suicidal campaign of manufacturing unlimited amounts of goods (and waste).

The rethinking about work that inevitably must take place could well be done by the presently existing elites, and women may find that men have made the key decisions without them. The new structures of work to be devised in the next two decades (part of whose character will be determined by the need to have much *less* work of many kinds) could still perpetuate the sexist system intact—confining women to the role of parasitical, deferring helper. This can be prevented from happening only if women invade the world of work now, even while it is still "alienating," with a militant feminist consciousness.

6. In what way do you envisage the struggle for women's liberation: (a) in the framework of a revolutionary/political organization or (b) exclusively in the women's movement?

It is good news whenever a radical political organization supports the cause of women—particularly when the organization is one, like the Black Panthers, that had been notorious for its blatant sexism. But I am not optimistic about the long-term benefits of such support. The alliance

seems more natural than it really is. Revolutionary struggle usually does tend to enfranchise women as historical
agents and to override sexist stereotypes in a quick, dra-
matic way. Think of what women have done (have been
"allowed" to do) in the Commune, the Russian revolution,
the French and Italian resistance during World War II,
the struggle to create the State of Israel, the Cuban revolution, the thirty years of Vietnamese liberation struggle,
the Palestinian guerrilla movement, the urban guerrilla
movements in Latin America—in relation to what women
were allowed to do (thought capable of doing) in each of
these societies just before the start of armed struggle. But
the enfranchisement is only temporary. After the struggle
ends, whether in victory or defeat, women are inevitably
demobilized rapidly and encouraged to return to their
traditional, passive, ahistorical roles. (Later their participation will be ignored or glossed over by historians and
ideologists—as, for instance, in France, where there is an
astonishing silence today about the numerous fighters
and martyrs of the Resistance who were women. If their
deeds are told at all, they will be fitted into imagery that
confirms the leadership of men, as in that eminently sexist
recent Chinese film ostensibly made to honor and praise
the women soldiers in Mao's army in the 1930s, *The Red
Detachment of Women*.)

To break radically with sexual stereotypes, even if just
temporarily, seems to come easily to political radicals only
when they engage in insurrection, in "people's war," in
guerrilla struggle, or in underground resistance to foreign

occupation. In situations that fall short of military-type urgency, the treatment of women in radical political organizations is in fact anything but exemplary. Despite their often-proclaimed feminist "views," the internal life of almost all radical organizations, in or out of power—from the official communist parties to the new Left and semi-anarchist groups active since the 1960s—uncritically condones and promotes all sorts of sexist "habits."

Thus, the present wave of feminism was born out of the painful awakening of women in the largest radical student organization in America in the 1960s to the fact that they were being treated like second-class members. Women were never listened to with the same seriousness at meetings; it was always women members who were asked (or volunteered) to take the minutes, or to leave a meeting in progress to go into the kitchen to make coffee. Often chivalrously protected by their men comrades from police violence during demonstrations, they were invariably excluded from positions of leadership. To be sure, the complacent sexism of radical organizations has lessened somewhat, at least in America, precisely because of the protest these women made. At first only an isolated, ridiculed minority, they heralded a new level of consciousness on the part of many women—which, having started in America, is now belatedly spreading (though in a tamer and more limited way) to Western Europe. In the 1970s, women seeking to liberate themselves and other women can find more allies than ever among radical men. But working within existing revolutionary organizations is not enough. At this point, it is not even central.

Now and for some time to come, I think, the primary role must be played by women's movements. However many radical men can now be counted as allies (and they are not *that* numerous), women have to conduct the main part of the struggle themselves. Women must form groups in each class, each occupation, each community, to sustain and encourage different levels of struggle and emerging consciousness. (For example: all-women professional collectives—of doctors who will treat only women patients, of lawyers and accountants who will handle only women clients—as well as all-women rock groups, farms, filmmaking crews, small businesses, and so forth.) Politically, women will not find a militant voice until they organize in groups which they lead—just as Blacks did not find their true political militancy as long as they were represented mainly by integrated organizations, which meant, in practice, being led by benevolent, well-educated, liberal whites. One of the purposes of political action is to educate those who stage the action. At the present point of women's political underdevelopment, working with men (even sympathetic men) slows down the process by which women learn how to be politically mature.

Women have to learn, first of all, how to talk to one another. Like Blacks (and other colonized peoples), women have trouble organizing, are not easily disposed to respect one another and to take one another seriously. They are used to leadership, support, and approval by men. It is therefore all the more important that they do learn to organize politically by themselves, and try to reach other women. Their mistakes are at least *their* mistakes.

More generally: people who favor women working for their liberation in concert with men tacitly deny the realities of women's oppression. Such a policy ensures that all struggle on behalf of women will be moderate and, ultimately, co-optable. It is to arrange, in advance, that nothing "radical" will happen, that the consciousness of women will not change in a profound way. For integrated actions, those taken alongside of men, necessarily limit the freedom of women to think "radically." The sole chance women have to effect that deep change in their consciousness required for their liberation is by organizing separately. Consciousness changes only through confrontation, in situations in which appeasement is not possible.

Thus, there are certain activities that only all-women's groups can—or will want to—perform. Only groups composed entirely of women will be diversified enough in their tactics, and sufficiently "extreme." Women should lobby, demonstrate, march. They should take karate lessons. They should whistle at men in the streets, raid beauty parlors, picket toy manufacturers who produce sexist toys, convert in sizeable numbers to militant lesbianism, operate their own free psychiatric and abortion clinics, provide feminist divorce counseling, establish makeup withdrawal centers, adopt their mothers' family names as their last names, deface billboard advertising that insults women, disrupt public events by singing in honor of the docile wives of male celebrities and politicians, collect pledges to renounce alimony and giggling, bring lawsuits for defamation against the mass-circulation "women's magazines," conduct telephone harassment campaigns against male psychiatrists who have sexual relations with their women patients, organize beauty contests for men, put up feminist candidates for all public offices. Though no single action is necessary, the "extremist" acts are valuable in themselves, because they help women to raise their own consciousness. And, however much people claim to be shocked or put off by such acts, their rhetoric *does* have a positive effect upon the silent majority. Performed by even a small minority, this guerrilla theater forces millions to become defensive about hitherto barely conscious sexist attitudes, accustoming them to the idea that these attitudes are at least not self-evident. (I do not exclude the utility of real guerrilla violence as well.)

Undeterred by the fear of confirming sexist clichés (e.g., women as creatures of emotion, incapable of being detached, objective), militant groups must commit themselves to behavior that does violate the stereotypes of femininity. A common way of reinforcing the political passivity of women has been to say they will be more effective and influential if they act with "dignity," if they don't violate decorum, if they remain charming. Women should show their contempt for this form of intimidation disguised as friendly advice. Women will be much more effective politically if they are rude, shrill, and—by sexist standards—"unattractive." They will be met with ridicule, which they should do more than bear stoically. They should, indeed, welcome it. Only when their acts are described as "ridiculous" and their demands are dismissed as "exaggerated" and "unreasonable" can militant women be sure they are on the right track.

7. And in this case, what will be the long-term and the short-term objectives?

The important difference is not between short-term and long-term objectives but, as I have already indicated, between objectives which are reformist (or liberal) and those which are radical. From suffrage onward, most of the objectives that women have sought have been reformist.

An example of the difference. To demand that women receive equal pay for equal work is reformist; to demand that women have access to all jobs and professions, without exception, is radical. The demand for equal wages does not attack the system of sexual stereotyping. Paying a woman the same wages a man gets *if* she holds the same job he does establishes a merely formal kind of equity. When roughly half the people doing every kind of job are women, when all forms of employment and public responsibility become fully coeducational, sexual stereotyping will end—not before.

In underlining this difference once again, I am not suggesting that the reformist gains are negligible. They are eminently worth struggling for—as evidenced by the fact that these demands are, for most people, too "radical." Most of the reformist demands are far from being granted. In that slow procession toward fulfilling the reformist demands, the communist countries have taken a clear lead. Next, but well behind them in terms of the degree of "liberal" enlightenment of public policy, come the capitalist countries with a Protestant background, notably Sweden, Denmark, England, Holland, the United States, Canada, and New Zealand. Lagging far behind to the rear are those countries with a Catholic cultural base, like France, Italy, Spain, Portugal, Mexico, and the countries of Central and South America—where married women cannot buy and dispose of property without the signature of their husbands; and where the right to divorce, not to mention the legality of abortion, remains fiercely contested. And still further behind the Latin countries, almost out of sight, are the countries with a Muslim culture—where women are still subjected to ferociously strict forms of social segregation, economic exploitation, and sexual surveillance. . . .

Despite the cultural unevenness with which the situation of women is being ameliorated, I would predict that most of the reformist demands will be granted in most countries by the end of the century. My point is that then the struggle will have only begun. The granting of these demands can leave intact all the oppressive and patronizing attitudes that make women into second-class citizens. Women have to feel, and learn to express, their anger.

Women must start making concrete demands—first

of all upon themselves and then upon men. For a start, women can note their acceptance of full adult status by symbolic acts, like not changing their last names when they marry. They can wean themselves from the enslaving concern with their personal appearance by which they consent to make themselves into objects. (By giving up makeup, and the reassuring ministrations of beauty parlors, they symbolically renounce the narcissism and vanity that are, insultingly, deemed normal in women.) They can refuse the rituals of male gallantry which dramatize their inferior position and convert it into a seduction. As often as not women should light men's cigarettes for them, carry their suitcases, and fix their flat tires. Even the trivial acts by which women ignore preassigned "feminine" roles have weight, helping to educate both women and men. They are the necessary prologue to any serious consideration on the part of women of the institutional framework for their liberation. This thinking must coincide with the creation of experimental institutions run by women, for women—living collectives, work collectives, schools, day-care centers, medical centers—which will embody the solidarity of women, their increasingly politicized consciousness, and their practical strategies for outwitting the system of sexual stereotyping.

The liberation of women has both short-term and long-term political meaning. Changing the status of women is not only a political objective in itself but prepares for (as well as constitutes part of) that radical change in the structure of consciousness and society, which is what I understand by revolutionary socialism. It is not simply that the liberation of women need not wait for the advent of socialism, so defined. It cannot wait.

I do not think socialism can triumph unless big victories for feminism have been won beforehand. The liberation of women is a necessary preparation for building a just society—not the other way around, as Marxists always claim. For if it does happen the other way around, women are likely to find their liberation a fraud. Should the transformation of society according to revolutionary socialism be undertaken without a prior militant independent women's movement, women will find that they have merely passed from the hegemony of one oppressive moral ethic to another.

8. Do you consider that the family is an obstacle for the liberation of woman?

Certainly the modern "nuclear family" operates to oppress women. And little consolation is to be had by considering other shapes that the family is known to have taken in the past and has today outside the societies of "European" type. Virtually *all* known forms of the family define women in ways that subordinate them to men—keeping them within the "home" while investing public power exclusively in the hands of men, who organize in all-male groups outside the family. In the chronology of human lives, the family is the first and psychologically the most irrefutable school for sexism. It is as small children, through the systematically contrasting ways in which girls and boys are treated (dressed, talked to, praised, punished), that the norms of dependency and narcissism are instilled in girls. Growing up, children learn the different expectations they may have for themselves from the models of mother and father: the fundamentally dissimilar geography of commitment that women and men make to family life.

The family is an institution organized around the exploitation of women as full-time inhabitants of the family's space. Hence, for women to work means relieving at least some part of their oppression. Working at a paid job, any job, a woman is no longer just a family creature. But she can still continue to be exploited, as a now part-time family creature still saddled with nearly full-time duties. Women who have gained the freedom to go out into "the world" but still have the responsibility for marketing, cooking, cleaning, and the children when they return from work have simply doubled their labor. This is the plight of almost all married working women in both capitalist and communist countries. (The oppressiveness of women's double load is particularly stark in the Soviet Union: with more diversity in the jobs open to women than in, say, the United States; with its consumer-society style of life just getting underway; and with hardly any "service" facilities.) Even when the wife holds down a job that is as honorable or as physically tiring as her husband's, when they both come home it still seems natural to the husband (and usually to the wife) that he rest while she prepares the dinner and cleans up afterward. Such exploitation will continue, even with the rising number of women entering the labor force, as long as their work so rarely challenges the notion of the "feminine" role.

Because most jobs that women get are conceived to be suited to their "feminine" aptitudes, most men and women experience no contradiction between that "woman's job" and the traditionally "feminine" arts (assistant, nurse, cook) that women are expected to exercise at home. Only when all sorts of jobs are filled by many women will it no longer seem natural to a husband to let his wife do all or most of the housework. What appear to be two quite different demands must be made jointly: that the range of employment no longer be determined along the lines of sexual identity, and that men share fully in the traditionally "feminine" work of domestic life. Both demands encounter intense resistance. Men find both demands embarrassing, threatening, though they seem to be made slightly less uncomfortable these days by the first than by the second—demonstrating that the grammar of family life (like language itself) is the most intense and stubborn fortress of sexist assumptions.

In an arrangement of family life which would not oppress women, men will take part in all domestic activities. (And women will be expected to give considerable time to "outside" obligations that have nothing to do with their families.) But the solution involves more than adjusting the degree of participation of men, the ideal being an equal sharing of all chores and responsibilities. These activities must themselves be rethought. The family does not have to be a sealed-off molecule, all of whose activities belong to "it." Many domestic tasks would be more efficiently and pleasantly carried out in a communal space—as they were in premodern societies. There is no genuine benefit in each family having (if it could) its private babysitter or maid; that is, freelance women hired to share or take over a wife's unpaid, unofficial servant role. Similarly, there is no reason (besides selfishness and fear) for each family to have its own washing machine, car, dishwasher, television set, and so forth. While private human (mostly female) domestic service is disappearing, except for the extremely rich, as countries pass from premodern economies to industrialization and consumerism, private mechanical services proliferate. Most of the new mechanical servants and services whose acquisition by the "individual" family is the primary article of faith of the consumer society could well be the common property of groups of families—thus reducing unnecessary duplication of labor; restraining competition, acquisitiveness; lessening waste. Democratizing family tasks is one of the steps necessary to change the oppressive definitions of the role of wife and husband, mother and father. It will also help break down the walls constructed in all modern industrial societies that separate one tiny family from another, thereby putting such devastating psychological strains on the members of each family.

The modern "nuclear" family is a psychological and moral disaster. It is a prison of sexual repression, a playing field of inconsistent moral laxity, a museum of possessiveness, a guilt-producing factory, and a school of selfishness. Yet despite the frightful price its members pay in anxiety and a backlog of murderous feelings, the modern family does allow some positive experiences. Particularly in capitalist society today, as Juliet Mitchell has pointed out, the family is often the only place where something approximating unalienated personal relations (of warmth, trust, dialogue, uncompetitiveness, loyalty, spontaneity, sexual pleasure, fun) are still permitted. It is no accident that one of the slogans of capitalist society, the form of society which promotes the greatest alienation in work and all communal bonds, is the sanctity of the family. (By the family is meant, though never said, the patriarchal "nuclear" family only.) Family life is the anachronistic reserve of exactly those "human-scale" values which industrial urban society destroys—but which it must somehow manage to conserve.

To survive, that is, to extract the maximum productivity and appetite for consumption from its citizenry, capitalism (and its cousin, Russian-style communism) must continue to grant a limited existence to the values of nonalienation. Thus it awards these values a privileged or protected status in an institution, the family, that is economically and politically innocuous. This is the ideological secret behind the very form of the modern nuclear family: a family unit too small in numbers, too stripped down, too confined in its living space (archetypally, the three-or four-room city apartment) to be viable as an economic unit or politically connected with sources of power. Early in the modern era, the home lost its ancient role as a site of altars and ritual; religious functions came to be entirely monopolized by "churches," whose activities the family members leave the house to attend as *individuals*. Since the late eighteenth century, the family has been forced to cede its right to educate (or not educate) its children to the centralized nation-state, which operates "public schools" that the children of each family are legally obliged to attend as *individuals*. The nuclear family, also known as the basic family, is the useless family—an ideal invention of urban industrial society. Its function is just that: to be useless, to be a refuge. Deprived of all economic, religious, and educational functions, the family exists solely as a source of emotional warmth in a cold world.

The glorification of the family is not only a piece of rank hypocrisy; it reveals an important structural contradiction in the ideology and workings of capitalist society. The ideological function of the modern family is manipulative—more accurately, self-manipulative. This does not mean we can dismiss what goes on in family life as entirely fraudulent. Genuine values are incarnated in the nuclear family. Indeed, were it not for even that poor form of family life that flourishes today, people would lead far more alienated lives than they already do. But the strategy will not work indefinitely. The contradiction between the values family life is charged with preserving and the values promoted by industrial mass society as a whole is, ultimately, an untenable one. Families are, in fact, less and less able to perform well this assigned task, the task which justifies the family in its modern form. The function of the family as ethical museum in industrial society is deteriorating; even there, "human-scale" values are leaking away. Industrial mass society stores the values of nonalienation in a safe place, an institution that is (by definition) apolitical. But no place is safe. The acids of the world "outside" are so strong that the family is becoming increasingly poisoned, more and more contaminated by society—which intrudes directly, for instance, in the homogenized voices of the television set in every living room.

To advocate "destroying" the family, because it is authoritarian, is a facile cliché. The vice of family life throughout history is not its authoritarianism, but that authority per se is founded on relations of ownership. Husbands "own" wives; parents "own" their children. (This is only one of the many similarities between the status of women and the status of children. Thus the sex whose members are *defined* as adult, and therefore as physically responsible for themselves, gallantly forces "women and children first" off sinking ships. In Spain, no married woman may hold a job, open a bank account, apply for a passport, or sign a contract without her husband's written permission—just like a child. Women, like children, have essentially the status of minors; they are wards of their husbands, as children are the wards of their parents.) Even the modern nuclear family in its liberalized Northern European and North American form is still based, though less blatantly so, on treating women and children as property.

The family based on ownership is the target: people should not be treated as property; adults should not be treated as minors. But some forms of authority make sense in family life. The question is what kind of authority, which depends on what the base of its legitimacy is. The restructuring of the family required for the emancipation of women means subtracting from the authority available to family arrangements one of its principal forms of legitimacy: the authority that men have over women. Although the family is the institution in which the oppression of women is originally incarnated, eliminating this oppression will not dissolve the family. Nor will a nonsexist family be without *any* idea of legitimate authority. When family arrangements are no longer a hierarchy dictated by sex roles, they will still have certain hierarchical features dictated by differences in age. A nonsexist family will not be completely unstructured, though it will be "open."

Precisely because the family is a singular institution— the only institution that modern society insists on defining as "private"—reconstructing the family is an extremely delicate project, and less amenable to the kind of advance planning for change that one can apply to other institutions. (What to do about schools, for instance, in order to make them nonsexist, as well as less authoritarian in other ways, is much clearer.) The reconstruction of family life must be part of the construction of new, but still small-scale, forms of community. This is where the women's movement can be particularly useful, by bringing into existence, within the context of today's society, alternative institutions that will pioneer the development of a new praxis of group life.

In any case, nothing can be done about the family by fiat. And, undoubtedly, some form of family life will continue. What is desirable is not to destroy the family, but to destroy the opposition (particularly entrenched in capitalist countries) between "home" and "the world." This opposition is decadent. It is oppressive to women (and children), and it stifles or drains off those communitarian—sororal and fraternal—feelings on which a new society could be built.

9. What place do you give to the right to abortion on demand among the objectives of women's struggle?

The legalization of abortion is a reformist demand—like the removal of the stigma on unwed mothers and so-called illegitimate children, and the establishment of free childcare facilities for working mothers—and as such, suspect. History shows that the anger of women, when channeled into pressing reformist demands only, is all too easily defused (as happened to the movement organized around suffrage in England and America once women were finally given the vote after World War I). Such reforms tend to narrow, and then abruptly disperse, militant energies. It also can be argued that they directly bolster the repressive system, by ameliorating some of its hardships. Contrary to what is felt with such passion, particularly in Latin countries, it's more plausible to suppose that gaining the right to have an abortion—like the right to divorce and to purchase contraceptives legally and cheaply—will help conserve the present system of marriage and the family. In this way, such reforms actually reinforce the power of men, indirectly confirming the licentious sexuality, exploitative of women, that is considered normal in this society.

These reforms do nevertheless correspond to the concrete, immediate needs of hundreds of millions of women—all but the rich and privileged. Ameliorating their condition can, given a proper theoretical consciousness in the women's movement, lead to other demands. Much of the value of struggling for goals of such limited, questionable political weight depends on where the struggle is taking place. As a rule, the harder the struggle is, the greater is the chance of politicizing it. Thus, to campaign for the legalizing of contraceptives and abortions has a larger political dimension in Italy or Argentina than it does in Norway or Australia. In itself, the right to abortion has no serious political content at all—despite its extreme desirability on humanitarian and ecological grounds. It becomes a valuable demand, however, when taken as a step in a chain of demands, and actions, which can mobilize and move forward the awareness of large numbers of women who have not yet begun to think consciously about their oppression. Nothing in the situation of women will be changed when any one of these rights is won. The fact that divorce is virtually impossible to get in Spain, while it is easy to get in Mexico, does not make the situation of women in Mexico substantially better than it is in Spain. But the struggle for these rights can be an important step in preparing for a more profound level of struggle.

10. How do you, who are precisely a liberated woman, experience the attitude of men toward you?

I would never describe myself as a liberated woman. Of course, things are never as simple as *that*. But I have always been a feminist.

When I was five years old, I daydreamed about becoming a biochemist and winning the Nobel Prize. (I had just read a biography of Madame Curie.) I stuck with chemistry until the age of ten, when I decided I would become a doctor. At fifteen, I knew I was going to be a writer. That is to say: from the beginning it never even occurred to me that I might be prevented from doing things in "the world" because I was born female. Perhaps because I spent most of my sickly childhood reading and in my chemistry laboratory in the empty garage, growing up in a very provincial part of the United States with a family life so minimal that it could be described as subnuclear, I was curiously innocent of the very existence of a barrier. When, at fifteen, I left home to go to a university, and then took up various careers, the relations that I had with men in my professional life seemed to me, with some exceptions, cordial and untroubled. So I went on not knowing there was a problem. I didn't even know I was a feminist, so unfashionable was that point of view at the time, when I married at the age of seventeen and kept my own name; it seemed to me an equally "personal" act of principle on my part, when I divorced my husband seven years later, to have indignantly rejected my lawyer's automatic bid for alimony, even though I was broke, homeless, and jobless at that moment and I had a six-year-old child to support.

Now and then, people I met would allude to the supposed difficulties of being both independent and a woman; I was always surprised—and sometimes annoyed, because, I thought, they were being obtuse. The problem didn't exist for me—except in the envy and resentment I occasionally felt from other women, the educated, jobless, home-stranded wives of the men with whom I worked. I was conscious of being an exception, but it hadn't ever seemed hard to be an exception; and I accepted the advantages I enjoyed as my right. I know better now.

My case is not uncommon. Not so paradoxically, the position of a "liberated" woman in a liberal society where the vast majority of women are *not* liberated can be embarrassingly easy. Granted a good dose of talent and a certain cheerful or merely dogged lack of self-consciousness, one can even escape (as I did) the initial obstacles and derision that are likely to afflict a woman who insists on autonomy. It will not seem so hard for such a woman to lead an independent life; she may even reap some professional advantages from being a woman, such as greater visibility. Her good fortune is like the good fortune of a few Blacks in a liberal but still racist society. Every liberal grouping (whether political, professional, or artistic) needs its token woman.

What I have learned in the last five years—helped by the women's movement—is to situate my own experience in a certain *political* perspective. My good fortune is really beside the point. What does it prove? Nothing.

Any already "liberated" woman who complacently accepts her privileged situation participates in the oppression of other women. I accuse the overwhelming majority of women with careers in the arts and sciences, in the liberal professions, and in politics of doing just that.

I have often been struck by how misogynistic most successful women are. They are eager to say how silly, boring, superficial, or tiresome they find other women, and how much they prefer the company of men. Like most men, who basically despise and patronize women, most "liberated" women don't like or respect other women. If they don't fear them as sexual rivals, they fear them as professional rivals—wishing to guard their special status as women admitted into largely all-male professional worlds. Most women who pass as being "liberated" are shameless Uncle Toms, eager to flatter their men colleagues, becoming their accomplices in putting down other, less accomplished women, dishonestly minimizing the difficulties they themselves have run into because of being women. The implication of their behavior is that all women can do what they have done, if only they would exert themselves; that the barriers put up by men are flimsy;

that it is mainly women themselves who hold themselves back. This simply is not true.

The first responsibility of a "liberated" woman is to lead the fullest, freest, and most imaginative life she can. The second responsibility is her solidarity with other women. She may live and work and make love with men. But she has no right to represent her situation as simpler, or less suspect, or less full of compromises than it really is. Her good relations with men must not be bought at the price of betraying her sisters.

(1973)

A Woman's Beauty

Put-Down or Power Source?

For the Greeks, beauty was a virtue: a kind of excellence. Persons then were assumed to be what we now have to call—lamely, enviously—*whole* persons. If it did occur to the Greeks to distinguish between a person's "inside" and "outside," they still expected that inner beauty would be matched by beauty of the other kind. The well-born young Athenians who gathered around Socrates found it quite paradoxical that their hero was so intelligent, so brave, so honorable, so seductive—and so ugly. One of Socrates's main pedagogical acts was to be ugly—and teach those innocent, no doubt splendid-looking disciples of his how full of paradoxes life really was.

They may have resisted Socrates's lesson. We do not. Several thousand years later, we are more wary of the enchantments of beauty. Being beautiful no longer speaks, presumptively, for the worth of a whole person. We not only split off—with the greatest facility—the "inside" (character, intellect) from the "outside" (looks); but we are actually surprised when someone who is beautiful is also intelligent, talented, good.

It was principally the influence of Christianity that deprived beauty of the central place it had in classical ideals of human excellence. By limited excellence (*virtus* in Latin) to *moral* virtue only, Christianity set beauty adrift—as an alienated, arbitrary, superficial enchantment. And beauty has continued to lose prestige. For close to two centuries it has become a convention to attribute beauty to only one of the two sexes: the sex which, however Fair, is always Second. Associating beauty with women has put beauty even further on the defensive, morally.

A beautiful woman, we say in English. But a handsome man. "Handsome" is the masculine equivalent of—and refusal of—a compliment which has accumulated certain demeaning overtones, by being reserved for women only. That one can call a man "beautiful" in French and in Italian suggests that Catholic countries—unlike those countries shaped by the Protestant version of Christianity—still retain some vestiges of the pagan admiration for beauty. But the difference, if one exists, is of degree only. In every modern country that is Christian or post-Christian, women *are* the beautiful sex—to the detriment of the notion of beauty as well as of women.

To be called beautiful is thought to name something essential to women's character and concerns. (In contrast to men—whose essence is to be strong, or effective, or competent.) It does not take someone in the throes of advanced feminist awareness to perceive that the way women are taught to be involved with beauty encourages narcissism, reinforces dependence and immaturity. Everybody (women and men) knows that. For it is "everybody," a whole society, that has identified being feminine with caring about how one *looks*. (In contrast to being masculine—which is identified with caring about what one *is* and *does* and only secondarily, if at all, about how one looks.) Given these stereotypes, it is no wonder that beauty enjoys, at best, a rather mixed reputation.

It is not, of course, the desire to be beautiful that is wrong but the obligation to be—or to try. What is accepted by most women as a flattering idealization of their sex is a way of making women feel inferior to what they actually are—or normally grow to be. For the ideal of beauty is administered as a form of self-oppression. Women are taught to see their bodies in *parts*, and to evaluate each part separately. Breasts, feet, hips, waistline, neck, eyes, nose, complexion, hair, and so on—each in turn is submitted to an anxious, fretful, often despairing scrutiny. Even if some pass muster, some will always be found wanting. Nothing less than perfection will do.

In men, good looks is a whole, something taken in at a glance. It does not need to be confirmed by giving measurements of different regions of the body; nobody encourages a man to dissect his appearance, feature by feature. As for perfection, that is considered trivial—almost unmanly. Indeed, in the ideally good-looking man a small imperfection or blemish is considered positively desirable. According to one movie critic (a woman) who is a declared

Robert Redford fan, it is having that cluster of skin-colored moles on one cheek that saves Redford from being merely a "pretty face." Think of the depreciation of women—as well as of beauty—that is implied in that judgment.

"The privileges of beauty are immense," said Cocteau. To be sure, beauty is a form of power. And deservedly so. What is lamentable is that it is the only form of power that most women are encouraged to seek. This power is always conceived in relation to men; it is not the power to do but the power to attract. It is a power that negates itself. For this power is not one that can be chosen freely—at least, not by women—or renounced without social censure.

To preen, for a woman, can never be just a pleasure. It is also a duty. It is her work. If a woman does real work—and even if she has clambered up to a leading position in politics, law, medicine, business, or whatever—she is always under pressure to confess that she still works at being attractive. But insofar as she is keeping up as one of the Fair Sex, she brings under suspicion her very capacity to be objective, professional, authoritative, thoughtful. Damned if they do—women are. And damned if they don't.

One could hardly ask for more important evidence of the dangers of considering persons as split between what is "inside" and what is "outside" than that interminable half-comic, half-tragic tale, the oppression of women. How easy it is to start off by defining women as caretakers of their surfaces, and then to disparage them (or find them adorable) for being "superficial." It is a crude trap, and it has worked for too long. But to get out of the trap requires that women get some critical distance from that excellence and privilege which is beauty, enough distance to see how much beauty itself has been abridged in order to prop up the mythology of the "feminine." There should be a way of saving beauty *from* women—and *for* them.

(1975)

Beauty

How Will It Change Next?

The ideas which seem most expressive, and exercise the greatest powers of seduction, are basically self-contradictory. One such idea is freedom. Another is beauty, that over-rich brew of so many familiar opposites: the natural and the historical, the pristine and the artificial, the individual-izing and the conformist—even the beautiful and the ugly.

Beauty, thought to be something intuitively appre-hended (and appreciated), is associated with the natural. Yet it is overwhelmingly clear that beauty is a historical fact. Different cultures exhibit an astonishing spread of ideas about beauty. And it is among so-called primitive, or at any rate premodern, societies that beauty is most drasti-cally linked to artifice. Depilation of body hair, body paint-ing, ornamental scarring of the skin are among the tamer forms of basic dressing up, while some cultures practice more ambitious mutilations—to get lips like saucers, can-tilevered buttocks, crushed feet, and similar beauty ideals that we in turn find extravagantly, self-evidently ugly.

But all programs of beauty, even when they seem par-ticularly perverse or tenacious, are inherently fragile. Any culture's ideal of beauty, however artificial or however natural, will be modified by contact with another culture; and, in cases of cultural rape, a society may precipitously lose confidence in its own standards of beauty—as the statistics on eyelid-straightening operations performed in Japan since World War II attest.

Another paradox. Beauty is always thought to be "given." But, at the same time, it is understood to be acquired. Beauty is something that needs to be taken care of, that must be watched over, that can be enhanced: through exercise, the right diet, lotions and creams. Something that can, within limits, be created or faked: through makeup, flattering clothes. (The last resort is, of course, surgery.) Beauty is the raw material for the arts of beautification, for what has become, in our time, the beauty "industry." Beauty is thought of both as a gift—that some people are born beautiful and others not passes for one of nature's (or God's) ruder injustices—and a mode of self-improvement. Physical attractiveness is regarded both as the natural condition of women and as a goal they have to work at, and diligently pursue, to distinguish themselves from other women.

And this suggests still another paradox. To be beautiful makes one singular, exceptional. But to be beautiful also means measuring up to a norm or rule ("fashion"). The paradox is partly eased when one remembers that beauty is one of those ideas—like truth, like freedom—that gets its meaning from its always being contrasted (if only tacitly) with an adversary, negative idea. But it would be naïve to suppose that the "ugly" is the only opposite implied by the "beautiful." Indeed, according to the very logic of fashion, the beautiful often has to seem—at first—ugly. The implicit opposite of the "beautiful" is rather the "common," the "vulgar."

In matters of beauty we are all born country bumpkins. We learn what is beautiful—which means that beauty can be, and is, taught. But it is hardly a teaching that promotes egalitarian feelings. Beauty is a class system, operating within the sexist code; its ruthless rating procedures and intractable encouragement to feelings of superiority and inferiority persist in spite of (and maybe because of) a striking amount of upward and downward mobility. Beauty is endless social climbing—rendered particularly arduous by the fact that, in our society, the terms that confer membership in the aristocracy of beauty keep changing. At the top of the hierarchy are "stars" who monopolize the right to launch a *new* insolent idea of beauty—which is then taken up and imitated by large numbers of people.

Some of the changes in the idea of beauty aren't real changes. Often, seemingly different standards of beauty in fact celebrate the same values. When most Europeans and Americans—including women—worked outdoors, very white skin was a sine qua non of feminine beauty. Now that most people work indoors, it's bronzed skin that is attractive. The apparent change of beauty ideal conceals a perfect continuity of standard. What is prized in both pallor and suntan is a skin color that is not associated with toil—that signifies luxury, privilege, leisure. Another example. It is not because of some arbitrary shift of "taste" that the ideal feminine figure has been getting progressively leaner (particularly in the hips) over the last century. Because all societies throughout history have been under the lash of scarcity, so that most people never had enough to eat, it was usually plumpness (or even obesity) that seemed beautiful. In unprecedentedly affluent modern Europe and North America, where for the first time in history most people eat too much, it is distinguished to be thin.

That many standards of the beautiful are attached to what sets off the "few" from the "many" does not mean, however, that all ideas of beauty in our society are equivalent or that there is no change of any interesting kind. Beauty, as we know it, flourishes according to the imperatives of the consumer society: that is, to create needs that didn't exist before.

In the early stages of consumerism, when only a relatively small number of people are solicited, the standards can remain provocatively high, snobbish. Beauty is associated with fragility, inaccessibility, glamour, elegance. But as the number of customers for those needs is steadily enlarged, it is inevitable that the standard come down a little. Now we have less aristocratic, less melancholy, less intimidating models of beauty.

Sarah Bernhardt, Greta Garbo, Marlene Dietrich were the most celebrated of the *princesses lointaines*; and it would be hard to overestimate the hypnotic authority that their languid, static poses and perfect faces had over whole generations. Nothing remotely like that degree of fealty and imaginative submission was given to those late (too late) representatives of their race: plastic princesses like Grace Kelly and Catherine Deneuve, who are, for *my* taste, simply too beautiful. (In the cases of Deneuve and Kelly, their stalled or abandoned careers as stars suggest that being *that* beautiful is, in our generation, something of a handicap. A borderline case: Faye Dunaway, whose career has already faltered over the problem. In order to make it as a star, Dunaway has to seek roles that hide how beautiful she is.)

We have today more "natural," "healthier," more varied ideas of beauty, which emphasize activity rather than languidness. (Though the activities—romantic courtship, sports, vacationing—are still identified with leisure rather than work.) Beauty is no longer ideal; it is individualized. Presumably, this change makes clients of the beautiful feel less anxiety about not meeting impossibly high standards. But even in its relatively more accessible form, as standards of beauty appear to be becoming more democratic, they are still propagated by "stars."

Fashion sets a standard that is, by definition, high, probably too high; otherwise it would not be compelling. Yet those standards are, we are told, accessible to everyone. But how far can beauty be democratized—without losing its authority as an idea, its allure as a paradox? Probably, all democratizations of beauty in our culture are spurious: just another turn of fashion's wheel. Thus, fashion both exalts perfection and ostentatiously de-emphasizes it. Even the "natural" is a form of theater; it takes a lot of artifice to look "natural." It is probably no easier to model oneself on Lauren Hutton than on Sarah Bernhardt.

That current notions of beauty are both natural and more theatrical follows from the role that beauty and the beauty "industry" play in the consumer society. In China, the model *anti*-consumer society, there is no ideology of beauty at all. In the Soviet Union, an example of a society in the early stages of transition to consumerism, the ideology of beauty is either nonexistent or retrograde. The Soviets' first attempts at "fashion" not only seem frumpy and unpoetic by our standards but—what may amount to the same thing—reflect old-style bourgeois stereotypes about femininity. Russians seem (to our eyes) remarkably unselfconscious about ugliness—particularly fat, as one concludes from the display of unembarrassed ample flesh on beaches. The self-consciousness will come, as the consumer society gets underway, and will probably mean a step backward—at least temporarily—from the more egalitarian situation of women (at least in job roles) that currently prevails in the U.S.S.R. But it will be a long time (how many generations of affluence?) before the Russians are ready for a fanciful approach to the idea of beauty, the one perfected in our own advanced consumer society.

Beauty is, of course, a myth. The question is, what sort of myth. In the past two centuries, it has been a myth imprisoning to women—because it is exclusively associated with *them*. The idea of beauty that we inherit was invented by men (to buttress their own claims to superior, less superficial virtues) and is still largely administered by men. It is a system from which men scrupulously have exempted themselves.

But that is beginning to change. The last ten years have been the decade in which male beauty has come out of the closet. The myth of beauty seems, once more, to be going coed. Now, standards of beauty are being applied to men as well as women—with men consenting to be treated and treating themselves as sexual "objects," not just as virile hairy predators. To some extent, the recent tilt of beauty toward a single standard (at least among the young) seems to render the myth of beauty less reactionary—that is, less noxious for women.

To be sure, the taste for unisex beauty is not a truly radical change. Beauty, as a notion, still remains stamped by allusions to the "feminine"—even in the newly colonized androgynous world of male beauty. Thus, David Bowie's beauty derives from the extent to which he resembles—and comments on—the beauty of Katharine Hepburn. But masculine narcissism has other dimensions, another morality, other consequences than feminine narcissism. Society does not define caring for one's appearance as a duty for men. It can never be less than a choice—not (as for women) an obligation that is regarded as part of one's sexual identity.

At the moment when standards for men became more

dandyish, some women took up arms against the way the conventions of beauty reinforce the image of women as indolent, smooth-skinned, odorless, empty-headed, affable playthings. There was a flurry of revolt against makeup. Some women stopped shaving their legs. Fewer and fewer younger women patronized hairdressers. For women who decided that they did not have to tamper with themselves, did not have to be works of art in order to be beautiful, the beauty of women acquired a new, polemical meaning—as a feminist slogan.

Feminists affirmed that "women are beautiful" in the same defiant spirit that Afro-Americans proclaimed that "Black is beautiful." Women were recovering a suppressed freedom with respect to beauty, as Blacks were recovering a non-Caucasian standard of beauty, one more "natural" to them.

Feminism—which has been rather rough on the traditional hard sell of beauty to women, for all obvious and good reasons—has pushed for a beauty that is more "natural." But that idea still competes with other ideas of beauty that remain influential and moving. It is no accident that the feminist critique surfaced in a really effective and vivid way in the 1960s, a decade in which the richest and most central notion was "style." (By the triumph of "style" in the '60s I mean, of course, the validation of a *plurality* of styles.) According to the new permissive standards, ugly—freaky, eccentric—is beautiful. "Natural" is beautiful. But so is "unnatural." Fantasy proliferates. Change is a constant.

Modifications of the idea of beauty succeed each other

in an accelerating rhythm, so that it is fair to predict that no ideal of face or figure will last for a person's lifetime, or even get one through early adulthood without several major retoolings. (Anyone over thirty-five has already lived through several radical changes of beauty ideals: from the big breasts of the 1940s and early '50s to the boyish silhouette of the 1960s, from laboriously straightened hair to glorious Afros, etc.)

But perhaps more important than any specific recent change in the idea of beauty is the immense diffusion of awareness that beauty changes. What was once the specialized knowledge of anthropologists, historians of clothes, sociologists, and fashion professionals is now common knowledge. Everyone acknowledges the "relativity" of beauty: that different cultures construct beauty differently and that our own culture has a complex history of notions about the beautiful. Beauty is an idea that has entered the era of self-consciousness. Every idea of beauty that is proposed has as its subtext that it will not last: that it is only a "fashion."

In a sense, we can't take beauty as seriously as we once did. But now we are free to play with it. Hence, the cannibalizing of styles from the past that now makes high fashion virtually synonymous with irony. Clothes become costumes. The once awkwardly received fact of the influence of homosexual taste is now matter-of-factly accepted. In the age of innocence, beauty is conceived as a fixed, real value. We come after the age of innocence.

Everything now conspires to undermine the old, static

myth of beauty as something fixed. Expensively produced magazines that articulate and promote fashion contribute, inadvertently, to the demolition of the reactionary idea of beauty as much as do such sharp-eyed critics of the fashion industry as Blair Sabol. Both the cult of fashion and the feminist critique of it are undermining the stability of the beauty-myth. And increasing the beautiful. There seem to be more and more good-looking people around, in the societies touched by "fashion." The rapidity with which our ideas of beauty change is not just a by-product of the modern world's resources for ever quicker transmission of information. It itself produces a qualitative alteration in our idea of beauty, one that makes it less oppressive, more voluntary, and more of a turn-on.

Beauty continues to become more complicated, more self-conscious than ever and subject to chronic (if partly forced) change. Which—from the feminist point of view— may well be good news. And good news for aesthetes and sensualists as well. It would seem that, for once, the interests of moralists (of the feminist persuasion) and aesthetes coincide. Both have something to gain from the fact that it is now part of the *essence* of beauty that it change.

(1975)

Fascinating Fascism

First Exhibit. Here is a book of 126 splendid color photographs by Leni Riefenstahl, certainly the most ravishing book of photographs published anywhere in recent years. In the intractable mountains of the southern Sudan live about eight thousand aloof, godlike Nuba, emblems of physical perfection, with large, well-shaped, partly shaven heads, expressive faces, and muscular bodies that are depilated and decorated with scars; smeared with sacred gray-white ash, the men prance, squat, brood, wrestle on the arid slopes. And here is a fascinating layout of twelve black-and-white photographs of Riefenstahl on the back cover of *The Last of the Nuba*, also ravishing, a chronological sequence of expressions (from sultry inwardness to the grin of a Texas matron on safari) vanquishing the intractable march of aging. The first photograph was taken in 1927 when she was twenty-five and already a movie star, the most recent are dated 1969 (she is cuddling a naked African baby) and 1972 (she is holding a camera), and each of them shows some version of an ideal presence, a kind of imperishable beauty, like Elisabeth Schwarzkopf's, that only gets gayer and more metallic and healthier-looking with old age. And here is a biographical sketch of Riefenstahl on the dust jacket, and an introduction (unsigned) entitled "How Leni Riefenstahl came to study the Mesakin Nuba of Kordofan"—full of disquieting lies.

The introduction, which gives a detailed account of Riefenstahl's pilgrimage to the Sudan (inspired, we are told, by reading Hemingway's *The Green Hills of Africa* "one sleepless night in the mid-1950s"), laconically identifies the photographer as "something of a mythical figure as a filmmaker before the war, half-forgotten by a nation which chose to wipe from its memory an era of its history." Who (one hopes) but Riefenstahl herself could have thought up this fable about what is mistily referred to as "a nation" which for some unnamed reason "chose" to perform the deplorable act of cowardice of forgetting "an era"—tactfully left unspecified—"of its history"? Presumably, at least some readers will be startled by this coy allusion to Germany and the Third Reich.

Compared with the introduction, the jacket of the book is positively expansive on the subject of the photographer's career, parroting misinformation that Riefenstahl has been dispensing for the last twenty years.

It was during Germany's blighted and momentous 1930s that Leni Riefenstahl sprang to international fame as a film director. She was born in 1902, and her first devotion was to creative dancing. This led to her participation in silent films, and soon she was herself making—and starring in—her own talkies, such as *The Mountain* (1929).

These tensely romantic productions were widely admired, not least by Adolf Hitler, who, having attained power in 1933, commissioned Riefenstahl to make a documentary on the Nuremberg Rally in 1934.

It takes a certain originality to describe the Nazi era as "Germany's blighted and momentous 1930s," to summarize the events of 1933 as Hitler's "having attained power," and to assert that Riefenstahl, most of whose work was in its own decade correctly identified as Nazi propaganda, enjoyed "international fame as a film director," ostensibly like her contemporaries Renoir, Lubitsch, and Flaherty. (Could the publishers have let LR write the jacket copy herself? One hesitates to entertain so unkind a thought, although "her first devotion was to creative dancing" is a phrase few native speakers of English would be capable of.)

The facts are, of course, inaccurate or invented. Not only did Riefenstahl not make—or star in—a talkie called *The Mountain* (1929). No such film exists. More generally: Riefenstahl did not first simply participate in silent films and then, when sound came in, begin directing and starring in her own films. In all nine films she ever acted in, Riefenstahl was the star; and seven of these she did not direct. These seven films were: *The Holy Mountain* (*Der heilige Berg*, 1926), *The Big Jump* (*Der grosse Sprung*, 1927),

The Fate of the House of Habsburg (*Das Schicksal derer von Habsburg,* 1928), *The White Hell of Pitz Palü* (*Die weisse Hölle vom Piz Palü,* 1929)—all silents—followed by *Avalanche* (*Stürme über dem Montblanc,* 1930), *White Frenzy* (*Der weisse Rausch,* 1931), and *S.O.S. Iceberg* (*S.O.S. Eisberg,* 1932–1933). All but one were directed by Arnold Fanck, *auteur* of hugely successful Alpine epics since 1919, who made only two more films, both flops, after Riefenstahl left him to strike out on her own as a director in 1932. (The film not directed by Fanck is *The Fate of the House of Habsburg,* a royalist weepie made in Austria in which Riefenstahl played Marie Vetsera, Crown Prince Rudolf's companion at Mayerling. No print seems to have survived.)

Fanck's pop-Wagnerian vehicles for Riefenstahl were not just "tensely romantic." No doubt thought of as apolitical when they were made, these films now seem in retrospect, as Siegfried Kracauer has pointed out, to be an anthology of proto-Nazi sentiments. Mountain climbing in Fanck's films was a visually irresistible metaphor for unlimited aspiration toward the high mystic goal, both beautiful and terrifying, which was later to become concrete in Führer-worship. The character that Riefenstahl generally played was that of a wild girl who dares to scale the peak that others, the "valley pigs," shrink from. In her first role, in the silent *The Holy Mountain* (1926), that of a young dancer named Diotima, she is wooed by an ardent climber who converts her to the healthy ecstasies of Alpinism. This character underwent a steady aggrandizement. In her first sound film, *Avalanche* (1930), Riefenstahl is a mountain-possessed girl in love with a young meteorologist, whom she rescues when a storm strands him in his observatory on Mont Blanc.

Riefenstahl herself directed six films, the first of which, *The Blue Light* (*Das blaue Licht*, 1932), was another mountain film. Starring in it as well, Riefenstahl played a role similar to the ones in Fanck's films for which she had been so "widely admired, not least by Adolf Hitler," but allegorizing the dark themes of longing, purity, and death that Fanck had treated rather scoutishly. As usual, the mountain is represented as both supremely beautiful and dangerous, that majestic force which invites the ultimate affirmation of and escape from the self—into the brotherhood of courage and into death. The role Riefenstahl devised for herself is that of a primitive creature who has a unique relation to a destructive power: only Junta, the rag-clad outcast girl of the village, is able to reach the mysterious blue light radiating from the peak of Mount Cristallo, while other young villagers, lured by the light, try to climb the mountain and fall to their deaths. What eventually causes the girl's death is not the impossibility of the goal symbolized by the mountain but the materialist, prosaic spirit of envious villagers and the blind rationalism of her lover, a well-meaning visitor from the city.

The next film Riefenstahl directed after *The Blue Light* was not "a documentary on the Nuremberg Rally in 1934"—Riefenstahl made four nonfiction films, not two, as she has claimed since the 1950s and as most current whitewashing accounts of her repeat—but *Victory of the*

Faith (*Sieg des Glaubens*, 1933), celebrating the first National Socialist Party Congress held after Hitler seized power. Then came the first of two works which did indeed make her internationally famous, the film on the next National Socialist Party Congress, *Triumph of the Will* (*Triumph des Willens*, 1935)—whose title is never mentioned on the jacket of *The Last of the Nuba*—after which she made a short film (eighteen minutes) for the army, *Day of Freedom: Our Army* (*Tag der Freiheit: Unsere Wehrmacht*, 1935), that depicts the beauty of soldiers and soldiering for the Führer. (It is not surprising to find no mention of this film, a print of which was found in 1971; during the 1950s and 1960s, when Riefenstahl and everyone else believed *Day of Freedom* to have been lost, she had it dropped from her filmography and refused to discuss it with interviewers.)

The jacket copy continues:

> Riefenstahl's refusal to submit to Goebbels' attempt to subject her visualisation to his strictly propagandistic requirements led to a battle of wills which came to a head when Riefenstahl made her film of the 1936 Olympic Games, *Olympia*. This, Goebbels attempted to destroy; and it was only saved by the personal intervention of Hitler.
>
> With two of the most remarkable documentaries of the 1930s to her credit, Riefenstahl continued making films of her devising, unconnected with the rise of Nazi Germany, until 1941, when war conditions made it impossible to continue.

Her acquaintance with the Nazi leadership led to her arrest at the end of the Second World War: she was tried twice, and acquitted twice. Her reputation was in eclipse, and she was half forgotten—although to a whole generation of Germans her name had been a household word.

Except for the bit about her having once been a household word in Nazi Germany, not one part of the above is true. To cast Riefenstahl in the role of the individualist-artist, defying philistine bureaucrats and censorship by the patron state ("Goebbels' attempt to subject her visualisation to his strictly propagandistic requirements"), should seem like nonsense to anyone who has seen *Triumph of the Will*—a film whose very conception negates the possibility of the filmmaker's having an aesthetic conception independent of propaganda. The facts, denied by Riefenstahl since the war, are that she made *Triumph of the Will* with unlimited facilities and unstinting official cooperation (there was never any struggle between the filmmaker and the German minister of propaganda). Indeed, Riefenstahl was, as she relates in the short book about the making of *Triumph of the Will*, in on the planning of the rally—which was from the start conceived as the set of a film spectacle.* *Olympia*—a three-and-a-half-hour

* Leni Riefenstahl, *Hinter den Kulissen des Reichparteitag-Films* (Munich, 1935). A photograph on page 31 shows Hitler and Riefenstahl bending over some plans, with the caption: "The preparations for the Party Congress were made hand in hand with the preparations for the camera work." The

film in two parts, *Festival of the People (Fest der Völker)* and *Festival of Beauty (Fest der Schönheit)*—was no less an official production. Riefenstahl has maintained in interviews since the 1950s that *Olympia* was commissioned by the International Olympic Committee, produced by her own company, and made over Goebbels's protests. The truth is that *Olympia* was commissioned and entirely financed by the Nazi government (a dummy company was set up in Riefenstahl's name because it was thought unwise for the government to appear as the producer) and facilitated by Goebbels's ministry at every stage of the shooting;* even the plausible-sounding legend of Goebbels objecting to her footage of the triumphs of the Black American track star Jesse Owens is untrue. Riefenstahl worked for eighteen months on the editing, finishing in time so that the film could have its world premiere on April 29, 1938, in Berlin, as part of the festivities for Hitler's forty-ninth birthday; later that year *Olympia* was the principal German entry at the Venice Film Festival, where it won the Gold Medal.

---

rally was held on September 4–10; Riefenstahl relates that she began work in May, planning the film sequence by sequence, and supervising the construction of elaborate bridges, towers, and tracks for the cameras. In late August, Hitler came to Nuremberg with Viktor Lutze, head of the SA, "for an inspection and to give final instructions." Her thirty-two cameramen were dressed in SA uniforms throughout the shooting, "a suggestion of the Chief of Staff [Lutze], so that no one will disturb the solemnity of the image with his civilian clothing." The SS supplied a team of guards.
* See Hans Barkhausen, "Footnote to the History of Riefenstahl's 'Olympia,'" *Film Quarterly*, Fall 1974—a rare act of informed dissent amid the large number of tributes to Riefenstahl that have appeared in American and Western European film magazines during the last few years.

More lies: to say that Riefenstahl "continued making films of her devising, unconnected with the rise of Nazi Germany, until 1941." In 1939 (after returning from a visit to Hollywood, the guest of Walt Disney), she accompanied the invading Wehrmacht into Poland as a uniformed army war correspondent with her own camera team; but there is no record of any of this material surviving the war. After *Olympia* Riefenstahl made exactly one more film, *Tiefland* (*Lowland*), which she began in 1941—and, after an interruption, resumed in 1944 (in the Barrandov Film Studios in Nazi-occupied Prague), and finished in 1954. Like *The Blue Light, Tiefland* opposes lowland or valley corruption to mountain purity, and once again the protagonist (played by Riefenstahl) is a beautiful outcast. Riefenstahl prefers to give the impression that there were only two documentaries in a long career as a director of fiction films, but the truth is that four of the six films she directed were documentaries made for and financed by the Nazi government.

It is hardly accurate to describe Riefenstahl's professional relationship to and intimacy with Hitler and Goebbels as "her acquaintance with the Nazi leadership." Riefenstahl was a close friend and companion of Hitler's well before 1932; she was a friend of Goebbels, too: no evidence supports Riefenstahl's persistent claim since the 1950s that Goebbels hated her, or even that he had the power to interfere with her work. Because of her unlimited personal access to Hitler, Riefenstahl was precisely the only German filmmaker who was not responsible to the Film Office (Reichsfilmkammer) of Goebbels's ministry of propaganda. Last, it is misleading to say that Riefenstahl was "tried twice, and acquitted twice" after the war. What happened is that she was briefly arrested by the Allies in 1945 and two of her houses (in Berlin and Munich) were seized. Examinations and court appearances started in 1948, continuing intermittently until 1952, when she was finally "de-Nazified" with the verdict: "No political activity in support of the Nazi regime which would warrant punishment." More important: whether or not Riefenstahl deserved a prison sentence, it was not her "acquaintance" with the Nazi leadership but her activities as a leading propagandist for the Third Reich that were at issue.

The jacket copy of *The Last of the Nuba* summarizes faithfully the main line of the self-vindication which Riefenstahl fabricated in the 1950s and which is most fully spelled out in the interview she gave to *Cahiers du Cinéma* in September 1965. There she denied that any of her work was propaganda—calling it cinema verité. "Not a single scene is staged," Riefenstahl says of *Triumph of the Will*. "Everything is genuine. And there is no tendentious commentary for the simple reason that there is no commentary at all. It is *history—pure history*." We are a long way from that vehement disdain for "the chronicle-film," mere "reportage" or "filmed facts," as being unworthy of the event's "heroic style" which is expressed in her book on the making of the film.*

---

* If another source is wanted—since Riefenstahl now claims (in an interview in the German magazine *Filmkritik*, August 1972) that she didn't

Although *Triumph of the Will* has no narrative voice, it does open with a written text heralding the rally as the redemptive culmination of German history. But this opening statement is the least original of the ways in which the film is tendentious. It has no commentary because it doesn't need one, for *Triumph of the Will* represents an already achieved and radical transformation of reality: history become theater. How the 1934 Party convention was staged was partly determined by the decision to produce *Triumph of the Will*—the historic event serving as the set of a film which was then to assume the character of an

---

write a single word of *Hinter den Kulissen des Reichparteitag-Films*, or even read it at the time—there is an interview in the *Völkischer Beobachter*, August 26, 1933, about her filming of the 1933 Nuremberg rally, where she makes similar declarations.

Riefenstahl and her apologists always talk about *Triumph of the Will* as if it were an independent "documentary," often citing technical problems encountered while filming to prove she had enemies among the Party leadership (Goebbels's hatred), as if such difficulties were not a normal part of filmmaking. One of the more dutiful reruns of the myth of Riefenstahl as mere documentarist—and political innocent—is the *Filmguide to "Triumph of the Will"* published in the Indiana University Press Filmguide Series, whose author, Richard Meram Barsam, concludes his preface by expressing his "gratitude to Leni Riefenstahl herself, who cooperated in many hours of interviews, opened her archive to my research, and took a genuine interest in this book." Well might she take an interest in a book whose opening chapter is "Leni Riefenstahl and the Burden of Independence," and whose theme is "Riefenstahl's belief that the artist must, at all costs, remain independent of the material world. In her own life, she has achieved artistic freedom, but at a great cost." Etc.

As an antidote, let me quote an unimpeachable source (at least he's not here to say he didn't write it)—Adolf Hitler. In his brief preface to *Hinter den Kulissen*, Hitler describes *Triumph of the Will* as "a totally unique and incomparable glorification of the power and beauty of our Movement." And it is.

authentic documentary. Indeed, when some of the footage of Party leaders at the speakers' rostrum was spoiled, Hitler gave orders for the shots to be refilmed; and Streicher, Rosenberg, Hess, and Frank histrionically repledged their fealty to the Führer weeks later, without Hitler and without an audience, on a studio set built by Speer. (It is altogether correct that Speer, who built the gigantic site of the rally on the outskirts of Nuremberg, is listed in the credits of *Triumph of the Will* as architect of the film.) Anyone who defends Riefenstahl's films as documentaries, if documentary is to be distinguished from propaganda, is being ingenuous. In *Triumph of the Will*, the document (the image) not only is the record of reality but is one reason for which the reality has been constructed, and must eventually supersede it.

The rehabilitation of proscribed figures in liberal societies does not happen with the sweeping bureaucratic finality of the *Soviet Encyclopedia*, each new edition of which brings forward some hitherto unmentionable figures and lowers an equal or greater number through the trap door of nonexistence. Our rehabilitations are smoother, more insinuative. It is not that Riefenstahl's Nazi past has suddenly become acceptable. It is simply that, with the turn of the cultural wheel, it no longer matters. Instead of dispensing a freeze-dried version of history from above, a liberal society settles such questions by waiting for cycles of taste to distill out the controversy.

The purification of Leni Riefenstahl's reputation of its Nazi dross has been gathering momentum for some time, but it has reached some kind of climax this year, with Riefenstahl the guest of honor at a new cinéphile-controlled film festival held in the summer in Colorado and the subject of a stream of respectful articles and interviews in newspapers and on TV, and now with the publication of *The Last of the Nuba*. Part of the impetus behind Riefenstahl's recent promotion to the status of a cultural monument surely owes to the fact that she is a woman. The 1973 New York Film Festival poster, made by a well-known artist who is also a feminist, showed a blond doll-woman whose right breast is encircled by three names: Agnes Leni Shirley. (That is, Varda, Riefenstahl, Clarke.) Feminists would feel a pang at having to sacrifice the one woman who made films that everybody acknowledges to be first-rate. But the strongest impetus behind the change in attitude toward Riefenstahl lies in the new, ampler fortunes of the idea of the beautiful.

The line taken by Riefenstahl's defenders, who now include the most influential voices in the avant-garde film establishment, is that she was always concerned with beauty. This, of course, has been Riefenstahl's own contention for some years. Thus the *Cahiers du Cinéma* interviewer set Riefenstahl up by observing fatuously that what *Triumph of the Will* and *Olympia* "have in common is that they both give form to a certain reality, itself based on a certain idea of form. Do you see anything peculiarly German about this concern for form?" To this, Riefenstahl answered:

I can simply say that I feel spontaneously attracted by everything that is beautiful. Yes: beauty, harmony. And perhaps this care for composition, this aspiration to form is in effect something very German. But I don't know these things myself, exactly. It comes from the unconscious and not from my knowledge. . . . What do you want me to add? Whatever is purely realistic, slice-of-life, which is average, quotidian, doesn't interest me. . . . I am fascinated by what is beautiful, strong, healthy, what is living. I seek harmony. When harmony is produced I am happy. I believe, with this, that I have answered you.

That is why *The Last of the Nuba* is the last, necessary step in Riefenstahl's rehabilitation. It is the final rewrite of the past; or, for her partisans, the definitive confirmation that she was always a beauty freak rather than a horrid propagandist.*
Inside the beautifully produced book, photographs of the perfect, noble tribe. And on the jacket, photographs of "my perfect German woman" (as Hitler called Riefenstahl), vanquishing the slights of history, all smiles.

---

* This is how Jonas Mekas (*The Village Voice*, October 31, 1974) salutes the publication of *The Last of the Nuba*: "Riefenstahl continues her celebration—or is it a search?—of the classical beauty of the human body, the search which she began in her films. She is interested in the ideal, in the monumental." Mekas in the same paper on November 7, 1974: "And here is my own final statement on Riefenstahl's films: If you are an idealist, you'll see idealism in her films; if you are a classicist, you'll see in her films an ode to classicism; if you are a Nazi, you'll see in her films Nazism."

Admittedly, if the book were not signed by Riefenstahl, one would not necessarily suspect that these photographs had been taken by the most interesting, talented, and effective artist of the Nazi era. Most people who leaf through *The Last of the Nuba* will probably see it as one more lament for vanishing primitives—the greatest example remains Lévi-Strauss in *Tristes Tropiques* on the Bororo Indians in Brazil—but if the photographs are examined carefully, in conjunction with the lengthy text written by Riefenstahl, it becomes clear that they are continuous with her Nazi work. Riefenstahl's particular slant is revealed by her choice of this tribe and not another: a people she describes as acutely artistic (everyone owns a lyre) and beautiful (Nuba men, Riefenstahl notes, "have an athletic build rare in any other African tribe"); endowed as they are with "a much stronger sense of spiritual and religious relations than of worldly and material matters," their principal activity, she insists, is ceremonial. *The Last of the Nuba* is about a primitivist ideal: a portrait of a people subsisting in a pure harmony with their environment, untouched by "civilization."

All four of Riefenstahl's commissioned Nazi films—whether about Party congresses, the Wehrmacht, or athletes—celebrate the rebirth of the body and of community, mediated through the worship of an irresistible leader. They follow directly from the films of Fanck in which she starred and her own *The Blue Light*. The Alpine fictions are tales of longing for high places, of the challenge and ordeal of the elemental, the primitive; they are about the vertigo before power, symbolized by the majesty and beauty of mountains. The Nazi films are epics of achieved community, in which everyday reality is transcended through ecstatic self-control and submission; they are about the triumph of power. And *The Last of the Nuba*, an elegy for the soon-to-be extinguished beauty and mystic powers of primitives whom Riefenstahl calls "her adopted people," is the third in her triptych of fascist visuals.

In the first panel, the mountain films, heavily dressed people strain upward to prove themselves in the purity of the cold; vitality is identified with physical ordeal. For the middle panel, the films made for the Nazi government: *Triumph of the Will* uses overpopulated wide shots of massed figures alternating with close-ups that isolate a single passion, a single perfect submission: in a temperate zone clean-cut people in uniforms group and regroup, as if they were seeking the perfect choreography to express their fealty. In *Olympia*, the richest visually of all her films (it uses both the verticals of the mountain films and the horizontal movements characteristic of *Triumph of the Will*), one straining, scantily clad figure after another seeks the ecstasy of victory, cheered on by ranks of compatriots in the stands, all under the still gaze of the benign Super-Spectator, Hitler, whose presence in the stadium consecrates this effort. (*Olympia*, which could as well have been called *Triumph of the Will*, emphasizes that there are no easy victories.) In the third panel, *The Last of the Nuba*, the almost naked primitives, awaiting the final ordeal of their proud heroic community, their imminent extinction, frolic and pose under the scorching sun.

It is Götterdämmerung time. The central events in Nuba society are wrestling matches and funerals: vivid encounters of beautiful male bodies and death. The Nuba, as Riefenstahl interprets them, are a tribe of aesthetes. Like the henna-daubed Masai and the so-called Mudmen of New Guinea, the Nuba paint themselves for all important social and religious occasions, smearing on a white-gray ash which unmistakably suggests death. Riefenstahl claims to have arrived "just in time," for in the few years since these photographs were taken the glorious Nuba have been corrupted by money, jobs, clothes. (And, probably, by war—which Riefenstahl never mentions, since what she cares about is myth not history. The civil war that has been tearing up that part of the Sudan for a dozen years must have scattered new technology and a lot of detritus.)

Although the Nuba are Black, not Aryan, Riefenstahl's portrait of them evokes some of the larger themes of Nazi ideology: the contrast between the clean and the impure, the incorruptible and the defiled, the physical and the mental, the joyful and the critical. A principal accusation against the Jews within Nazi Germany was that they were urban, intellectual, bearers of a destructive, corrupting "critical spirit." The book bonfire of May 1933 was launched with Goebbels's cry: "The age of extreme Jewish intellectualism has now ended, and the success of

the German revolution has again given the right of way
to the German spirit." And when Goebbels officially for-
bade art criticism in November 1936, it was for having "typically Jewish traits of character": putting the head over the
heart, the individual over the community, intellect over
feeling. In the transformed thematics of latter-day fascism,
the Jews no longer play the role of defiler. It is "civilization" itself.

What is distinctive about the fascist version of the old
idea of the Noble Savage is its contempt for all that is re-
flective, critical, and pluralistic. In Riefenstahl's casebook
of primitive virtue, it is hardly—as in Lévi-Strauss—the
intricacy and subtlety of primitive myth, social organization, or thinking that is being extolled. Riefenstahl
strongly recalls fascist rhetoric when she celebrates the
ways the Nuba are exalted and unified by the physical or-
deals of their wrestling matches, in which the "heaving
and straining" Nuba men, "huge muscles bulging," throw
one another to the ground—fighting not for material
prizes but "for the renewal of the sacred vitality of the
tribe." Wrestling and the rituals that go with it, in Riefenstahl's account, bind the Nuba together. Wrestling

is the expression of all that distinguishes the Nuba
way of life. . . . Wrestling generates the most passionate loyalty and emotional participation in the team's
supporters, who are, in fact, the entire "non-playing"
population of the village. . . . Its importance as the

expression of the total outlook of the Mesakin and Korongo cannot be exaggerated; it is the expression in the visible and social world of the invisible world of the mind and of the spirit.

In celebrating a society where the exhibition of physical skill and courage and the victory of the stronger man over the weaker are, as she sees it, the unifying symbols of the communal culture—where success in fighting is the "main aspiration of a man's life"—Riefenstahl seems hardly to have modified the ideas of her Nazi films. And her portrait of the Nuba goes further than her films in evoking one aspect of the fascist ideal: a society in which women are merely breeders and helpers, excluded from all ceremonial functions, and represent a threat to the integrity and strength of men. From the "spiritual" Nuba point of view (by the Nuba Riefenstahl means, of course, males), contact with women is profane; but, ideal society that this is supposed to be, the women know their place.

The fiancées or wives of the wrestlers are as concerned as the men to avoid any intimate contact . . . their pride at being the bride or wife of a strong wrestler supersedes their amorousness.

Lastly, Riefenstahl is right on target with her choice as a photographic subject of a people who "look upon death as simply a matter of fate—which they do not resist or struggle against," of a society whose most enthusiastic and lavish ceremonial is the funeral. Viva la muerte.

It may seem ungrateful and rancorous to refuse to cut loose *The Last of the Nuba* from Riefenstahl's past, but there are salutary lessons to be learned from the continuity of her work as well as from that curious and implacable recent event—her rehabilitation. The careers of other artists who became fascists, such as Céline and Benn and Marinetti and Pound (not to mention those, like Pabst and Pirandello and Hamsun, who embraced fascism in the decline of their powers), are not instructive in a comparable way. For Riefenstahl is the only major artist who was completely identified with the Nazi era and whose work, not only during the Third Reich but thirty years after its fall, has consistently illustrated many themes of fascist aesthetics.

Fascist aesthetics include but go far beyond the rather special celebration of the primitive to be found in *The Last of the Nuba*. More generally, they flow from (and justify) a preoccupation with situations of control, submissive behavior, extravagant effort, and the endurance of pain; they endorse two seemingly opposite states, egomania and servitude. The relations of domination and enslavement take the form of a characteristic pageantry: the massing of groups of people; the turning of people into things; the multiplication or replication of things; and the grouping of people/things around an all-powerful, hypnotic leader-figure or force. The fascist dramaturgy centers on the orgiastic transactions between mighty forces and their puppets, uniformly garbed and shown in ever swelling numbers. Its choreography alternates between ceaseless motion and a congealed, static, "virile" posing. Fascist art glorifies surrender, it exalts mindlessness, it glamorizes death.

Such art is hardly confined to works labeled as fascist or produced under fascist governments. (To cite films only: Walt Disney's *Fantasia*, Busby Berkeley's *The Gang's All Here*, and Kubrick's *2001* also strikingly exemplify certain formal structures and themes of fascist art.) And, of course, features of fascist art proliferate in the official art of communist countries—which always presents itself under the banner of realism, while fascist art scorns realism in the name of "idealism." The tastes for the monumental and for mass obeisance to the hero are common to both fascist and communist art, reflecting the view of all totalitarian regimes that art has the function of "immortalizing" its leaders and doctrines. The rendering of movement in grandiose and rigid patterns is another element in common, for such choreography rehearses the very unity of the polity. The masses are made to take form, be design. Hence mass athletic demonstrations, a choreographed display of bodies, are a valued activity in all totalitarian countries; and the art of the gymnast, so popular now in Eastern Europe, also evokes recurrent features of fascist aesthetics: the holding in or confining of force, military precision.

In both fascist and communist politics, the will is staged publicly, in the drama of the leader and the chorus. What is interesting about the relation between politics and art under National Socialism is not that art was subordinated to political needs, for this is true of dictatorships both of the right and of the left, but that politics appropriated the rhetoric of art—art in its late romantic phase. (Politics is "the highest and most comprehensive art there is," Goebbels said in 1933, "and we who shape modern German policy feel ourselves to be artists . . . the task of art and the artist [being] to form, to give shape, to remove the diseased and create freedom for the healthy.") What is interesting about art under National Socialism are those features which make it a special variant of totalitarian art. The official art of countries like the Soviet Union and China aims to expound and reinforce a utopian morality. Fascist art displays a utopian aesthetics—that of physical perfection. Painters and sculptors under the Nazis often depicted the nude, but they were forbidden to show any bodily imperfections. Their nudes look like pictures in physique magazines: pinups which are both sanctimoniously asexual and (in a technical sense) pornographic, for they have the perfection of a fantasy. Riefenstahl's promotion of the beautiful and the healthy, it must be said, is much more sophisticated than this; and never witless, as it is in other Nazi visual art. She appreciates a range of bodily types—in matters of beauty she is not racist—and in *Olympia* she does show some effort and strain, with its attendant imperfections, as well as stylized, seemingly effortless exertions (such as diving, in the most admired sequence of the film).

In contrast to the asexual chasteness of official communist art, Nazi art is both prurient and idealizing. A utopian aesthetics (physical perfection; identity as a biological given) implies an ideal eroticism: sexuality converted into the magnetism of leaders and the joy of followers. The fascist ideal is to transform sexual energy into a "spiritual" force, for the benefit of the community. The erotic (that is, women) is always present as a temptation, with the most admirable response being a heroic repression of the sexual impulse. Thus Riefenstahl explains why Nuba marriages, in contrast to their splendid funerals, involve no ceremonies or feasts.

> A Nuba man's greatest desire is not union with a woman but to be a good wrestler, thereby affirming the principle of abstemiousness. The Nuba dance ceremonies are not sensual occasions but rather "festivals of chastity"—of containment of the life force.

Fascist aesthetics is based on the containment of vital forces; movements are confined, held tight, held in.

Nazi art is reactionary, defiantly outside the century's mainstream of achievement in the arts. But just for this reason it has been gaining a place in contemporary taste. The left-wing organizers of a current exhibition of Nazi painting and sculpture (the first since the war) in Frankfurt have found, to their dismay, the attendance excessively large and hardly as serious-minded as they had hoped. Even when flanked by didactic admonitions from Brecht and by concentration-camp photographs, what Nazi art reminds these crowds of is—other art of the 1930s, notably Art Deco. (Art Nouveau could never be a fascist style; it is, rather, the prototype of that art which fascism defines as decadent; the fascist style at its best is Art Deco, with its sharp lines and blunt massing of material, its petrified eroticism.) The same aesthetic responsible for the bronze colossi of Arno Breker—Hitler's (and, briefly, Cocteau's) favorite sculptor—and of Josef Thorak also produced the muscle-bound Atlas in front of Manhattan's Rockefeller Center and the faintly lewd monument to the fallen doughboys of World War I in Philadelphia's Thirtieth Street railroad station.

To an unsophisticated public in Germany, the appeal of Nazi art may have been that it was simple, figurative, emotional; not intellectual; a relief from the demanding complexities of modernist art. To a more sophisticated public, the appeal is partly to that avidity which is now bent on retrieving all the styles of the past, especially the most pilloried. But a revival of Nazi art, following the revivals of Art Nouveau, Pre-Raphaelite painting, and Art Deco, is most unlikely. The painting and sculpture are not just sententious; they are astonishingly meager as art. But precisely these qualities invite people to look at Nazi art with knowing and sniggering detachment, as a form of Pop Art.

Riefenstahl's work is free of the amateurism and naïveté

one finds in other art produced in the Nazi era, but it still promotes many of the same values. And the same very modern sensibility can appreciate her as well. The ironies of Pop sophistication make for a way of looking at Riefenstahl's work in which not only its formal beauty but its political fervor are viewed as a form of aesthetic excess. And alongside this detached appreciation of Riefenstahl is a response, whether conscious or unconscious, to the subject itself, which gives her work its power.

Triumph of the Will and *Olympia* are undoubtedly superb films (they may be the two greatest documentaries ever made), but they are not really important in the history of cinema as an art form. Nobody making films today alludes to Riefenstahl, while many filmmakers (including myself) regard Dziga Vertov as an inexhaustible provocation and source of ideas about film language. Yet it is arguable that Vertov—the most important figure in documentary films—never made a film as purely effective and thrilling as *Triumph of the Will* or *Olympia*. (Of course, Vertov never had the means at his disposal that Riefenstahl had. The Soviet government's budget for propaganda films in the 1920s and early 1930s was less than lavish.)

In dealing with propagandistic art on the left and on the right, a double standard prevails. Few people would admit that the manipulation of emotion in Vertov's later films and in Riefenstahl's provides similar kinds of exhilaration. When explaining why they are moved, most people are sentimental in the case of Vertov and dishonest in the case of Riefenstahl. Thus Vertov's work evokes a good deal of moral sympathy on the part of his cinéphile audiences all over the world; people consent to be moved. With Riefenstahl's work, the trick is to filter out the noxious political ideology of her films, leaving only their "aesthetic" merits. Praise of Vertov's films always presupposes the knowledge that he was an attractive person and an intelligent and original artist-thinker, eventually crushed by the dictatorship which he served. And most of the contemporary audience for Vertov (as for Eisenstein and Pudovkin) assumes that the film propagandists in the early years of the Soviet Union were illustrating a noble ideal, however much it was betrayed in practice. But praise of Riefenstahl has no such recourse, since nobody, not even her rehabilitators, has managed to make Riefenstahl seem even likable; and she is no thinker at all.

More important, it is generally thought that National Socialism stands only for brutishness and terror. But this is not true. National Socialism—more broadly, fascism—also stands for an ideal or rather ideals that are persistent today under the other banners: the ideal of life as art, the cult of beauty, the fetishism of courage, the dissolution of alienation in ecstatic feelings of community; the repudiation of the intellect; the family of man (under the parenthood of leaders). These ideals are vivid and moving to many people, and it is dishonest as well as tautological to say that one is affected by *Triumph of the Will* and *Olympia* only because they were made by a filmmaker of genius. Riefenstahl's films are still effective because, among other reasons, their longings are still felt, because their content is a romantic ideal to which many continue to be attached and which is expressed in such diverse modes of cultural dissidence and propaganda for new forms of community as the youth/rock culture, primal therapy, anti-psychiatry, Third World camp-following, and belief in the occult. The exaltation of community does not preclude the search for absolute leadership; on the contrary, it may inevitably lead to it. (Not surprisingly, a fair number of the young people now prostrating themselves before gurus and submitting to the most grotesquely autocratic discipline are former anti-authoritarians and anti-elitists of the 1960s.)

Riefenstahl's current de-Nazification and vindication as indomitable priestess of the beautiful—as a filmmaker and, now, as a photographer—do not augur well for the keenness of current abilities to detect the fascist longings in our midst. Riefenstahl is hardly the usual sort of aesthete or anthropological romantic. The force of her work being precisely in the continuity of its political and aesthetic ideas, what is interesting is that this was once seen so much more clearly than it seems to be now, when people claim to be drawn to Riefenstahl's images for their beauty of composition. Without a historical perspective, such connoisseurship prepares the way for a curiously absentminded acceptance of propaganda for all sorts of destructive feelings—feelings whose implications people are refusing to take seriously. Somewhere, of course, everyone knows that more than beauty is at stake in art like

Riefenstahl's. And so people hedge their bets—admiring this kind of art, for its undoubted beauty, and patronizing it, for its sanctimonious promotion of the beautiful. Backing up the solemn choosy formalist appreciations lies a larger reserve of appreciation, the sensibility of camp, which is unfettered by the scruples of high seriousness: and the modern sensibility relies on continuing trade-offs between the formalist approach and camp taste.

Art which evokes the themes of fascist aesthetic is popular now, and for most people it is probably no more than a variant of camp. Fascism may be merely fashionable, and perhaps fashion with its irrepressible promiscuity of taste will save us. But the judgments of taste themselves seem less innocent. Art that seemed eminently worth defending ten years ago, as a minority or adversary taste, no longer seems defensible today, because the ethical and cultural issues it raises have become serious, even dangerous, in a way they were not then. The hard truth is that what may be acceptable in elite culture may not be acceptable in mass culture, that tastes which pose only innocuous ethical issues as the property of a minority become corrupting when they become more established. Taste is context, and the context has changed.

II

Second Exhibit. Here is a book to be purchased at airport magazine stands and in "adult" bookstores, a relatively cheap paperback, not an expensive coffee-table item appealing to art lovers and the *bien-pensant* like *The Last of the Nuba*. Yet both books share a certain community of moral origin, a root preoccupation: the same preoccupation at different stages of evolution—the ideas that animate *The Last of the Nuba* being less out of the moral closet than the cruder, more efficient idea that lies behind *SS Regalia*. Though *SS Regalia* is a respectable British-made compilation (with a three-page historical preface and notes in the back), one knows that its appeal is not scholarly but sexual. The cover already makes that clear. Across the large black swastika of an SS armband is a diagonal yellow stripe which reads "Over 100 Brilliant Four-Color Photographs Only $2.95," exactly as a sticker with the price on it used to be affixed—part tease, part deference to censorship—on the cover of pornographic magazines, over the model's genitalia.

There is a general fantasy about uniforms. They suggest community, order, identity (through ranks, badges, medals, things which declare who the wearer is and what he has done: his worth is recognized), competence, legitimate authority, the legitimate exercise of violence. But uniforms are not the same thing as photographs of uniforms—which are erotic materials and photographs of SS uniforms are the units of a particularly powerful and widespread sexual fantasy. Why the SS? Because the SS was the ideal incarnation of fascism's overt assertion of the righteousness of violence, the right to have total power over others and to treat them as absolutely inferior. It was in the SS that this assertion seemed most complete, because they acted it out

in a singularly brutal and efficient manner; and because
they dramatized it by linking themselves to certain aesthetic standards. The SS was designed as an elite military
community that would be not only supremely violent
but also supremely beautiful. (One is not likely to come
across a book called "SA Regalia." The SA, whom the SS
replaced, were not known for being any less brutal than
their successors, but they have gone down in history as
beefy, squat, beerhall types; mere brownshirts.)

SS uniforms were stylish, well-cut, with a touch (but
not too much) of eccentricity. Compare the rather boring
and not very well cut American army uniform: jacket, shirt,
tie, pants, socks, and lace-up shoes—essentially civilian
clothes no matter how bedecked with medals and badges.
SS uniforms were tight, heavy, stiff and included gloves to
confine the hands and boots that made legs and feet feel
heavy, encased, obliging their wearer to stand up straight.
As the back cover of *SS Regalia* explains:

> The uniform was black, a colour which had impor-
> tant overtones in Germany. On that, the SS wore a
> vast variety of decorations, symbols, badges to distin-
> guish rank, from the collar runes to the death's-head.
> The appearance was both dramatic and menacing.

The cover's almost wistful come-on does not quite pre-
pare one for the banality of most of the photographs. Along
with those celebrated black uniforms, SS troopers were is-
sued almost American-army-looking khaki uniforms and

camouflage ponchos and jackets. And besides the photographs of uniforms, there are pages of collar patches, cuff bands, chevrons, belt buckles, commemorative badges, regimental standards, trumpet banners, field caps, service medals, shoulder flashes, permits, passes—few of which bear either the notorious runes or the death's-head; all meticulously identified by rank, unit, and year and season of issue. Precisely the innocuousness of practically all of the photographs testifies to the power of the image: one is handling the breviary of a sexual fantasy. For fantasy to have depth, it must have detail. What, for example, was the color of the travel permit an SS sergeant would have needed to get from Trier to Lübeck in the spring of 1944? One needs all the documentary evidence.

If the message of fascism has been neutralized by an aesthetic view of life, its trappings have been sexualized. This eroticization of fascism can be remarked in such enthralling and devout manifestations as Mishima's *Confessions of a Mask* and *Sun and Steel*, and in films like Kenneth Anger's *Scorpio Rising* and, more recently and far less interestingly, in Visconti's *The Damned* and Cavani's *The Night Porter*. The solemn eroticizing of fascism must be distinguished from a sophisticated playing with cultural horror, where there is an element of the put-on. The poster Robert Morris made for his recent show at the Castelli Gallery is a photograph of the artist, naked to the waist, wearing dark glasses, what appears to be a Nazi helmet, and a spiked steel collar, attached to which is a stout chain which he holds in his manacled, uplifted hands. Morris is said to have considered this to be the only image that still has any power to shock: a singular virtue to those who take for granted that art is a sequence of ever-fresh gestures of provocation. But the point of the poster is its own negation. Shocking people in the context also means inuring them, as Nazi material enters the vast repertory of popular iconography usable for the ironic commentaries of Pop Art. Still, Nazism fascinates in a way other iconography staked out by the Pop sensibility (from Mao Tsetung to Marilyn Monroe) does not. No doubt, some part of the general rise of interest in fascism can be set down as a product of curiosity. For those born after the early 1940s, bludgeoned by a lifetime's palaver, pro and con, about communism, it is fascism—the great conversation piece of their parents' generation—which represents the exotic, the unknown. Then there is a general fascination among the young with horror, with the irrational. Courses dealing with the history of fascism are, along with those on the occult (including vampirism), among the best attended these days on college campuses. And beyond this the definitely sexual lure of fascism, which *SS Regalia* testifies to with unabashed plainness, seems impervious to deflation by irony or overfamiliarity.

In pornographic literature, films, and gadgetry throughout the world, especially in the United States, England, France, Japan, Scandinavia, Holland, and Germany, the SS has become a referent of sexual adventurism. Much of the imagery of far-out sex has been placed under the sign of Nazism. Boots, leather, chains, Iron Crosses on gleaming torsos, swastikas, along with meat hooks and heavy motorcycles, have become the secret and most lucrative paraphernalia of eroticism. In the sex shops, the baths, the leather bars, the brothels, people are dragging out their gear. But why? Why has Nazi Germany, which was a sexually repressive society, become erotic? How could a regime which persecuted homosexuals become a gay turn-on?

A clue lies in the predilections of the fascist leaders themselves for sexual metaphors. Like Nietzsche and Wagner, Hitler regarded leadership as sexual mastery of the "feminine" masses, as rape. (The expression of the crowds in *Triumph of the Will* is one of ecstasy; the leader makes the crowd come.) Left-wing movements have tended to be unisex, and asexual in their imagery. Right-wing movements, however puritanical and repressive the realities they usher in, have an erotic surface. Certainly Nazism is "sexier" than communism (which is not to the Nazis' credit, but rather shows something of the nature and limits of the sexual imagination).

Of course, most people who are turned on by SS uniforms are not signifying approval of what the Nazis did, if indeed they have more than the sketchiest idea of what that might be. Nevertheless, there are powerful and growing currents of sexual feeling, those that generally go by the name of sadomasochism, which make playing at Nazism seem erotic. These sadomasochistic fantasies and practices are to be found among heterosexuals as well as homosexuals, although it is among male homosexuals that the eroticizing of Nazism is most visible. S-m, not swinging, is the big sexual secret of the last few years.

Between sadomasochism and fascism there is a natural link. "Fascism is theater," as Genet said.* As is sadomasochistic sexuality: to be involved in sadomasochism is to take part in a sexual theater, a staging of sexuality. Regulars of sadomasochistic sex are expert costumers and choreographers as well as performers, in a drama that is all the more exciting because it is forbidden to ordinary people. Sadomasochism is to sex what war is to civil life: the magnificent experience. (Riefenstahl put it: "Whatever is purely realistic, slice-of-life, which is average, quotidian, doesn't interest me.") As the social contract seems tame in comparison with war, so fucking and sucking come to

---

* It was Genet, in his novel *Funeral Rites*, who provided one of the first texts that showed the erotic allure fascism exercised on someone who was not a fascist. Another description is by Sartre, an unlikely candidate for these feelings himself, who may have heard about them from Genet. In *La Mort dans l'âme* (1949), the third novel in his four-part *Les Chemins de la liberté*, Sartre describes one of his protagonists experiencing the entry of the German army into Paris in 1940: "[Daniel] was not afraid, he yielded trustingly to those thousands of eyes, he thought 'Our conquerors!' and he was supremely happy. He looked them in the eye, he feasted on their fair hair, their sunburned faces with eyes which looked like lakes of ice, their slim bodies, their incredibly long and muscular hips. He murmured: 'How handsome they are!' . . . Something had fallen from the sky: it was the ancient law. The society of judges had collapsed, the sentence had been obliterated; those ghostly little khaki soldiers, the defenders of the rights of man, had been routed. . . . An unbearable, delicious sensation spread through his body; he could hardly see properly; he repeated, gasping, 'As if it were butter—they're entering Paris as if it were butter.' . . . He would like to have been a woman to throw them flowers."

seem merely nice, and therefore unexciting. The end to which all sexual experience tends, as Bataille insisted in a lifetime of writing, is defilement, blasphemy. To be "nice," as to be civilized, means being alienated from this savage experience—which is entirely staged.

Sadomasochism, of course, does not just mean people hurting their sexual partners, which has always occurred—and generally means men beating up women. The perennial drunken Russian peasant thrashing his wife is just doing something he feels like doing (because he is unhappy, oppressed, stupefied; and because women are handy victims). But the perennial Englishman in a brothel being whipped is re-creating an experience. He is paying a whore to act out a piece of theater with him, to reenact or reevoke the past—experiences of his schooldays or nursery which now hold for him a huge reserve of sexual energy. Today it may be the Nazi past that people invoke, in the theatricalization of sexuality, because it is those images (rather than memories) from which they hope a reserve of sexual energy can be tapped. What the French call "the English vice" could, however, be said to be something of an artful affirmation of individuality; the playlet referred, after all, to the subject's own case history. The fad for Nazi regalia indicates something quite different: a response to an oppressive freedom of choice in sex (and in other matters), to an unbearable degree of individuality; the rehearsal of enslavement rather than its reenactment.

The rituals of domination and enslavement being more and more practiced, the art that is more and more devoted

to rendering their themes, are perhaps only a logical extension of an affluent society's tendency to turn every part
of people's lives into a taste, a choice; to invite them to
regard their very lives as a (life) style. In all societies up
to now, sex has mostly been an activity (something to do,
without thinking about it). But once sex becomes a taste, it
is perhaps already on its way to becoming a self-conscious
form of theater, which is what sadomasochism is about:
a form of gratification that is both violent and indirect,
very mental.

Sadomasochism has always been the furthest reach of
the sexual experience: when sex becomes most purely sexual, that is, severed from personhood, from relationships,
from love. It should not be surprising that it has become
attached to Nazi symbolism in recent years. Never before was the relation of masters and slaves so consciously
aestheticized. Sade had to make up his theater of punishment and delight from scratch, improvising the décor and
costumes and blasphemous rites. Now there is a master
scenario available to everyone. The color is black, the material is leather, the seduction is beauty, the justification is
honesty, the aim is ecstasy, the fantasy is death.

(1974)

Feminism and Fascism

*An Exchange Between Adrienne Rich
and Susan Sontag*

To the Editors:

It was a strange experience to read Susan Sontag's critique [*NYR*, February 6] of Leni Riefenstahl and the eroticization of Nazism. I was forced to ask myself how the same mind had produced this brilliant essay, and the equally brilliant essay which appeared a year or two ago in *Partisan Review* ("The Third World of Women"). In her discussion of Riefenstahl and *SS Regalia* she seems often on the verge of making important sexual/political connections which, in fact, are never made.

First, there is a serious inaccuracy in her essay. She ascribes some of Riefenstahl's latter-day rehabilitation to "the fact that she is a woman," and states that "feminists would feel a pang at having to sacrifice the one woman who made films that everybody acknowledges to be first-rate." In fact, feminists (and on reading "The Third World of Women" one imagined Sontag not to dissociate herself from feminism) have in at least two cities protested the showing of Riefenstahl's films. At a women's film festival in Chicago, organized by both feminists and non-feminist filmmakers and critics, and financed by the *Chicago Tribune*, Riefenstahl had been invited to speak at a showing of *Triumph of the Will*; the invitation was withdrawn when members of the Chicago women's movement threatened to picket her. At the Telluride Festival in Colorado, organized not by feminists but by film-culture people, Riefenstahl's film was picketed by women. It is worth nothing that it is not Riefenstahl or Agnès Varda, but Leontine Sagan and Nelly Kaplan whose films (*Mädchen in Uniform*, an anti-authoritarian and lesbian film, and *A Very Curious Girl*) are most frequently chosen for showings at women's festivals, benefits, and coffeehouses.

It is, rather, the film culture that has "promoted Riefenstahl to the status of a cultural monument," as Sontag herself acknowledges later in her essay. The feminist movement has been passionately anti-hierarchal and anti-authoritarian. Feminists have also been justly alert to and critical of women who have "made it" in the patriarchy (and Nazi Germany was patriarchy in its purest, most elemental form). It is impossible not to recognize and mourn the pressures that drive token women to compromise their sisters and to serve misogynist and anti-human values. But there is a running criticism by radical feminists of male-identified "successful" women, whether they are artists, executives, psychiatrists, Marxists, politicians, or scholars.

The failed connections in Sontag's essay lead me to think back on "The Third World of Women." (This was a puzzling title, especially since "The Fourth World Manifesto," an important feminist paper by Barbara Burris and others, reprinted earlier in *Notes from the Third Year*, had delineated the idea of national culture as male culture, and of the imperialism toward women of "anti-imperialist" movements.) Sontag's lucid and beautifully reasoned *Partisan Review* piece begins to seem, after all, more of an intellectual exercise than the expression of a felt reality—her own—interpreted by a keen mind.

Many women, reading that piece, began to look in Sontag's new work for a serious reflection of feminist values. But there is an absence of integration or even continuity between "The Third World of Women" and, say, the film *Promised Lands* or the recent series of essays on photography. One is *not* looking for a "line" of propaganda or a "correct" position. One is simply eager to see this woman's mind working out of a deeper complexity, informed by emotional grounding; and this has not yet proven to be the case.

What *are* the themes of domination and enslavement, prurience and idealism, male physical perfection and death, "control, submissive behavior, and extravagant effort," "the turning of people into things," "vitality . . . identified with physical ordeal," the objectification of the body as separate from the emotions—what are these but masculinist, virilist, patriarchal values? Isn't the black-leather, brothel, ecstasy-in-death fantasy far less a lesbian fantasy than a fantasy of heterosexual males and the male homo-sexuals they oppress? And isn't the infatuation with these themes at this time possibly one aspect of the backlash of a false and threatened virility against the feminist rejection of those values, and their increasing rejection in the perva-sively changing consciousness of women who do not call themselves feminists?

I wish that Sontag could have carried her exploration of this cult beyond its encapsulation in a fad, or even in the phenomenon called fascism, and perceived it in the light of patriarchal history, sexuality, pornography, and power, in which the first people turned into things are always women, and female (negative) qualities are attributed to every dominated group as the excuse for domination. It is frustrating, and suggestive of the ways women's minds, as well as bodies, have been colonized, that this did not happen. And it is this kind of dissociation of one kind of knowledge from another which reinforces cultism and aesthetic compromise with the representatives of oppres-sion; precisely what Sontag herself was writing to deplore.

Adrienne Rich

New York City

Susan Sontag replies:

A quick answer to the puzzle Adrienne Rich has concocted in her flattering, censorious letter: "how the same mind had produced this brilliant essay, and the equally brilliant essay which appeared a year or two ago in *Partisan Review*

('The Third World of Women')." Easy. By addressing itself to a different problem, with the intention of making a different point.

Ms. Rich implies that I have made a slur on the feminist movement by suggesting that the vested interest and pride large numbers of women now have in all women of accomplishment have been propitious to Riefenstahl's remarkable comeback. Is that a "serious inaccuracy" on my part? If anything, I think that I understated the matter. The poster that Niki de Saint Phalle produced for the 1973 New York Film Festival (*Agnes Leni Shirley*) accurately reflected the contribution made by feminist consciousness at a certain level to whitewashing Riefenstahl.

As someone who has been contacted by the organizers of dozens of festivals and programs in North America, Western Europe, and Australia devoted to films by women, I can assure Adrienne Rich that, despite the rare occasions when the blue light doesn't get to shine in person (Chicago) or gets picketed when she does (Telluride), Riefenstahl's *films* are invariably selected and shown. Indeed, the multiplication of such events has gotten them shown frequently for the first time since the 1930s. It is simply untrue that Riefenstahl's films—along with Agnès Varda's—are often slighted, in favor of Leontine Sagan's superb film and Nelly Kaplan's mediocre ones. (Why, in heaven's name, exclude Agnès Varda?)

I didn't stick the blame for Riefenstahl's rehabilitation on female chauvinism first, then "acknowledge later" the real villain to be what Rich calls "the film culture." And I never meant to suggest that Riefenstahl's recent mutation from unperson to superstar has met with no catcalls— although, according to my informants, the conspicuous contingent of picketers at last summer's festival in Telluride, Colorado, were Jews from Denver, not feminists. I would assume that Riefenstahl offends some feminists (though I wish it were for a better reason than her being on that ominous-sounding enemies list, "male-identified 'successful' women"), just as her acclamation has troubled a few notables in the *cinéphile* establishment—for example, Amos Vogel, in an article in *The New York Times* (May 13, 1973). The important point is that the dissenters, whether in the women's movement or in "the film culture," are bucking a fait accompli brought about by trends running through our culture.

But my alleged misrepresentation of what takes place at specialized film festivals is not what most vexes Rich. Her main charge is that I have further let down the good cause by not exploring the feminist implications of my subject (those "failed connections"): namely, the roots of fascism in "patriarchal values." Virginia Woolf was, as far as I know, the first woman to make the connection, in *Three Guineas* (1938): "fighting the tyranny of the patriarchal state" is the same as "fighting the tyranny of the Fascist state." It is a rousing three-quarters truth when used in a general brief for feminism (what I was attempting in the text published in 1973 in *Partisan Review*, where Woolf is quoted). It is a skimpy half-truth if your subject is—as mine was in the *NYR* essay—fascism and fascist aesthetics.

Applied to a particular historical subject, the feminist passion yields conclusions which, however true, are extremely general. Like all capital moral truths, feminism is a bit simple-minded. That is its power and, as the language of Rich's letter shows, that is its limitation. Fascism must also be seen in the context of other—less perennial—problems. I tried to make a number of careful distinctions, and if my essay has some merit it lies in those distinctions.

Rich wants to persuade me that I'm haggling, unwilling to take the moral plunge. "What are these but masculinist, virilist, patriarchal values?" she asks. The trouble with *what-are-these-but* arguments is that they lead not just to a devaluation of the complexity of history, but to aspersions upon its very claim on our attention. Thus what I was discussing gets scaled down to a mere "cult" encapsulated in a "fad." Holding the subject at arm's length with a pair of verbal tongs, Rich refers to a "phenomenon called fascism" as if she were in some doubt about its reality—as indeed she is since, according to her view, all that epiphenomenal trash is nothing "in the light of" the real stuff, "patriarchal history."

Suppose, indeed, that "Nazi Germany was patriarchy in its purest, most elemental form." Where do we rate the Kaiser's Germany? Caesarist Rome? Confucian China? Fascist Italy? Victorian England? Ms. Gandhi's India? Macho Latin America? Arab sheikery from Mohammed to Qaddhafi and Faisal? Most of history, alas, is "patriarchal history." So distinctions will have to be made, and it is not possible to keep the feminist thread running through the explanations all the time. Virtually everything deplorable in human history furnishes material for a restatement of the feminist plaint (the ravages of the patriarchy, etc.), just as every story of a life could lead to a reflection on our common mortality and the vanity of human wishes. But if the point is to have meaning some of the time, it can't be made all the time.

It is this demand for an unremitting rhetoric, with every argument arriving triumphantly at a militant conclusion, which has prevented some feminists from properly appreciating that most remarkable of recent contributions to the feminist imagination of history, Elizabeth Hardwick's *Seduction and Betrayal*. A more specific reproach leveled against Hardwick's complex book is that it implicitly defends "elitist" values (like talent, genius), which are incompatible with the egalitarian ethics of feminism. I hear an echo of this self-righteous view when Rich characterizes the feminist movement as "passionately anti-hierarchal and anti-authoritarian."

That phrase, whether as a sample of "feminist values" or simply as a relic of the infantile leftism of the 1960s, seems to me sheer demagogy. However opposed I am to authority based on privileges of gender (and of race), I cannot imagine any form of human life or society without *some* forms of authority, of hierarchy. I am not against elders having some authority over young people, not against authority that is publicly accountable, not against all meritocracy. The hope of abolishing authority as such is part of a childish, sentimental fantasy about the human condition. Much of feminist rhetoric not only tends to reduce history to psychology but leaves one with a shallow psychology as well as a thinned-out sense of history. (*Vide* the criticisms made by Juliet Mitchell.)

Rich explains that she is "simply eager" to see my mind "working out of a deeper complexity, informed by emotional grounding." But it seems to me—from where I stand (sit, write)—that it's just because the complexity deepens and thickens that I am unable to put my shoulder to the feminist wheel in the fashion she would like me to. Despite her demurrer about "*not* looking for a 'line' of propaganda or a 'correct' position," this is exactly what she is doing. Why else would I be chided for not bending the immense subject of the image-world created by photography (the *NYR* essays) or a meditation on death and report on the current agony of the state of Israel (my recent film *Promised Lands*) to the concerns of feminism? But it is surely not treasonable to think that there are other goals than the depolarization of the two sexes, other wounds than sexual wounds, other identities than sexual identity, other politics than sexual politics—and other "anti-human values" than "misogynist" ones.

Even the feminist text that I wrote, for which Rich has such kind words at the beginning of her letter, is now revalued—downward—in view of my presumed failure to keep up feminist pressure at the center of my writing and filmmaking. Its very title now becomes "puzzling," suggesting unsuspected ignorance on my part of a *dernier cri* of feminist polemics, "The Fourth World Manifesto." (No puzzle. The editors of *Partisan Review*, after accepting my text—it had been turned down by *Ms.*, to which it was first submitted, as being too long and too abstruse—decided without consulting me to substitute for my boring title—"Reply to a Questionnaire"—their silly one.) Because my subsequent writings don't dot the *i*'s and cross the *t*'s of the feminist case, that *Partisan Review* text "begins to seem, after all, more of an intellectual exercise than the expression of a felt reality—her own—interpreted by a keen mind."

If Rich (hardly as ferociously as some of our sisters) is going to start baiting that heavy bear, the intellect, then I feel obliged to announce that anyone with a taste for "intellectual exercise" will always find in me an ardent defender. Truth has need of all kinds of exertion. Although I defy anyone to read what I wrote and miss its personal, even autobiographical character, I much prefer that the text be judged as an argument and not as an "expression" of anything at all, my sincere feelings included.

Adrienne Rich, whom I have always admired as poet and phenomenologist of anger, is a piker compared to some self-styled radical feminists, all too eager to dump the life of reason (along with the idea of authority) into the dustbin of "patriarchal history." Still, her well-intentioned letter does illustrate a persistent indiscretion of feminist rhetoric: anti-intellectualism. "One imagined Sontag not to dissociate herself from feminism," Rich observes. Right. But I do dissociate myself from that wing of feminism that promotes the rancid and dangerous antithesis between mind ("intellectual exercise") and emotion ("felt reality"). For precisely this kind of banal disparagement of the normative virtues of the intellect (its acknowledgement of the inevitable plurality of moral claims; the rights it accords, alongside passion, to tentativeness and detachment) is also one of the roots of fascism—what I was trying to expose in my argument about Riefenstahl.

The *Salmagundi* Interview

Interviewer: In "On Style," written in 1965, you wrote: "To call Leni Riefenstahl's *Triumph of the Will* and *Olympia* masterpieces is not to gloss over Nazi propaganda with aesthetic lenience . . . [but] these two films of Riefenstahl (unique among works of Nazi artists) transcend the categories of propaganda or even reportage. And we find ourselves—to be sure, rather uncomfortably—seeing 'Hitler' and not Hitler, the '1936 Olympics' and not the 1936 Olympics. Through Riefenstahl's genius as a filmmaker, the 'content' has—let us even assume, against her intentions—come to play a purely formal role." And you continue: "A work of art, so far as it is a work of art, cannot—whatever the artist's personal intention—advocate anything at all." Yet, in the Riefenstahl essay published a few months ago, you refer to *Triumph of the Will* as "a film whose very conception negates the possibility of the filmmaker's having an aesthetic conception independent of propaganda." At the very least, these two statements contrast with each other. Is there also a continuity between the two essays?

Sontag: A continuity, it seems to me, in that both statements illustrate the richness of the form-content distinction, as long as one is careful always to use it against itself. My point in 1965 was about the formal implications of content, while the recent essay examines the content implicit in certain ideas of form. One of the main assertions of "On Style" is that the formalist and the historicist approaches are not in competition with each other, but are complementary—and equally indispensable. That's where Riefenstahl comes in. Because her work speaks for values that have received an official seal of disapproval, it offers a vivid test of the exchanges between form and content. Knowing that *Triumph of the Will* and *Olympia* might be considered exceptions to the general argument I was making about the ways in which content functions as form, it seemed necessary to point out that even those films also illustrate the process whereby—as in any other bold and complex work of art—content functions as form. I wasn't discussing the complementary process, how form functions as content. When I set out, early this year, to treat Riefenstahl's work at some length, and with *that* approach, I arrived at an analysis that was simply more interesting, as well as more concrete—and that rather overwhelms the summary as well as formalist use I had made of her work in 1965. The paragraph about Riefenstahl in "On Style" is correct—as far as it goes. It just doesn't go very far. While it is true that her films in some sense transcend the propaganda for which they are the vehicle, their specific qualities show how their aestheticizing conception is itself identical with a certain brand of propaganda.

I'm still working with the thesis about the relation of art to the moral sense that is advanced in "On Style." But my understanding of the moral services that works of art perform is less abstract than it was in 1965. And I know more about totalitarianism and about the aesthetics with which it is compatible, which it actually generates, than I did then. One of the experiences that made me more interested in the, so to speak, "contentual" implications of form (without lessening my interest in the formal implications of content) was seeing—three years after I wrote "On Style"—several of the mass spectacle films made in China in the 1960s. One film led to another, inside my head—from *The East Is Red* to, say, Eisenstein's *Alexander Nevsky*, Walt Disney's *Fantasia*, the choreographed patterning of bodies as objects in Busby Berkeley musicals, Kubrick's *2001*. What these films exemplify is a major form of the modern aesthetic imagination which—as I've learned since the Riefenstahl essay was published—Siegfried Kracauer had explored as early as 1927, in an essay called "The Mass Ornament," and Walter Benjamin had summed up a few years later, when he described fascism as an aestheticization of political life.

It's not enough to say that an aesthetics is, or eventually becomes, a politics. What aesthetics? What politics? The key to understanding "fascist aesthetics," I think, is seeing that a "communist aesthetics" is probably a contradiction in terms. Hence, the mediocrity and staleness of the art promoted in communist countries. And when official art in the Soviet Union and China isn't resolutely old-fashioned, it is, objectively, fascist. Unlike the ideal communist society, which is totally didactic—turning every institution into a school—the fascist ideal is to mobilize everybody into a kind of national *Gesamtkunstwerk*: making the whole society into a theater. This is the most far-reaching way in which aesthetics becomes a politics. It becomes a politics of the lie. As Nietzsche said, "To experience a thing as beautiful means: to experience it necessarily wrongly." In the nineteenth century, ideologues of provocation and transvaluation like Nietzsche and Wilde expounded on "the aesthetic view of the world," one of whose superiorities was that it was supposed to be the most generous and large-spirited view, a form of civility, beyond politics. The evolution of fascism in the twentieth century has taught us that they were wrong. As it turns out, "the aesthetic view of the world" is extremely hospitable to many of the uncivilized ideas and dissociated yearnings that were made explicit in fascism, and which also have great currency in our consumer culture. Yet it is clear—China has made it very clear—that the moralism of *serious* communist societies not only wipes out the autonomy of the aesthetic but makes it impossible to produce art (in the modern sense) at all. A six-week trip to China in 1973 convinced me—if I needed convincing—that the autonomy of the aesthetic is something to be protected, and cherished, as indispensable nourishment to intelligence. But a decade-long residence in the 1960s, with its inexorable conversion of moral and political radicalisms into "style," has convinced me of the perils of overgeneralizing the aesthetic view of the world.

I would still argue that a work of art, qua work of art, cannot advocate anything. But since no work of art is in fact only a work of art, it's often more complicated than that. In "On Style" I was trying to recast the truths expressed in Wilde's calculatedly outrageous preface to *The Picture of Dorian Gray* and Ortega y Gasset's more sober overstatement of the same polemic against philistinism in *The Dehumanization of Art*—by not tacitly separating or actually opposing—as Wilde and Ortega do—aesthetic and moral response. Ten years after "On Style," this is still the position I write from. But I have more historical flesh on my bones now. Though I continue to be as besotted an aesthete and as obsessed a moralist as I ever was, I've come to appreciate the limitations—and the indiscretion—of generalizing either the aesthete's or the moralist's view of the world without a much denser notion of historical context. Since you've been quoting me to myself, let me quote myself back to you. I say in that essay of 1965 that "awareness of style as a problematic and isolable element in a work of art has emerged in the audience for art only at certain historical moments—as a front behind which other issues, ultimately ethical and political, are being debated." The essays I've been writing recently are attempts to take that point further, to make it concrete—as it applies to my own work, as well as to that of others.

Interviewer: When the poet Adrienne Rich attacked the essay on Riefenstahl for disregarding feminist values, you replied: "Applied to a particular historical subject, the feminist passion yields conclusions which, however true, are extremely general. . . . Most of history, alas, is 'patriarchal history.' So distinctions will have to be made. . . . Virtually everything deplorable in human history furnishes material for a restatement of the feminist plaint . . . just as every story of a life could lead to a reflection on our common mortality and the vanity of human wishes. But if the point is to have meaning some of the time, it can't be made all the time."* What are the times when the point should be made? Are there certain events, or "movements," or works of art that are more reasonable subjects for feminist criticism?

Sontag: I want armies of women and men to be pointing out the omnipresence of sexist stereotypes in the language, behavior, and imagery of our society. If that's what you mean by feminist criticism, then whenever it's practiced—and however coarsely—it's always of some value. But I'd like to see a few platoons of intellectuals who are also feminists doing their bit in the war against misogyny in their own way, letting the feminist implications be residual or implicit in their work, without risking being charged by their sisters with desertion. I don't like party lines. They make for intellectual monotony and bad prose. Let me put it very simply, though not—I hope—too plaintively. There are many intellectual tasks, and different levels of discourse. If there *is* a question of appropriateness, it's not because some events or works of art are

* "Feminism and Fascism: An Exchange," *The New York Review of Books*, Vol. XXII, No. 4, March 20, 1975.

more "reasonable" targets, but because people who reason in public have—and ought to exercise—options about how many and how complex are the points they want to make. And where, in what form, and to what audience they make them. Rich complained that I had failed to say that Nazi Germany was, after all, the culmination of a sexist and patriarchal society. She was assuming, of course, that the values of Riefenstahl's films were Nazi values. So was I. That's why I wanted to discuss the question: in *what* sense does Riefenstahl's work embody Nazi values? *Why* are these films—and *The Last of the Nuba*—interesting and persuasive? I think it was permissible to assume that the audience for whom I wrote my essay is aware of the derogation of women not only in Nazi ideology, but in the main tradition of German letters and thought from Luther to Nietzsche to Freud and Jung.

It's not the appropriateness of feminist criticism which needs to be rethought, but its level—its demands for intellectual simplicity, advanced in the name of ethical solidarity. These demands have convinced many women that it is undemocratic to raise questions about "quality"—the quality of feminist discourse, if it is sufficiently militant, and the quality of works of art, if these are sufficiently warm-hearted and self-revealing. Hatred of the intellect is one of the recurrent themes of modernist protest in art and in morals. Though actually quite inimical to effective political action, it seems like a political statement. Both avant-garde art and feminism have made large use of, and sometimes seem to be parodies of, the languages of failed political movements. As advanced art, in the 1910s, inherited the rhetoric of Anarchism (and baptized it Futurism), feminism, in the late 1960s, inherited another political rhetoric on the wane, that of *gauchisme*. One common denominator of New Left polemics was its zeal for pitting hierarchy against equality, theory against practice, intellect (cold) against feeling (warm). Feminists have tended to perpetuate these philistine characterizations of hierarchy, theory, and intellect. What was denounced in the 1960s as bourgeois, repressive, and elitist was discovered to be phallocratic, too. That kind of secondhand militancy may appear to serve feminist goals in the short run. But it means a surrender to callow notions of art and of thought and the encouragement of a genuinely repressive moralism.

Interviewer: In 1967 you wrote a long, admiring essay on Ingmar Bergman's *Persona*.* It has since become common to attack Bergman as a technically reactionary force in world cinema. Feminist critics complain that his films regularly project "negative" images of women which promise no useful encouragement to people in need of positive identity images. Do you share any of these views of Bergman as a reactionary artist, aesthetically or politically?

Sontag: I am extremely reluctant to attack anyone as a reactionary artist. That's the weapon of the repressive and ignorant officialdom in you-know-which countries, where "reactionary" is also associated with a kind of pessimistic content or (using the phrase you cite) with not

* In *Styles of Radical Will*, Farrar, Straus and Giroux, 1969.

providing "positive images." Being very attached to the benefits of pluralism in the arts and of factionalism in politics, I've grown allergic to the words "reactionary" and "progressive." Such judgments always support ideological conformity, encourage intolerance—even if they aren't originally formulated to do that. As for Bergman, I'd say that anyone who reduces his work to its neo-Strindbergian views of women has jettisoned the idea of art and of complex standards of judgment. (If correctness of attitude counted most, Abram Room's *Bed and Sofa*, full of appealing feminist intuitions, would be a greater film than Pudovkin's macho epic *Storm over Asia*.)

The harsh indictment of Bergman simply inverts the slack standards that prevail in much of feminist criticism. To those critics who rate films according to whether they make moral reparations, it must seem snobbish to cavil about the low quality of most recent movies made by women which do convey positive images. And what's happening when an attack on someone for not supplying "useful encouragement to people" is bolstered by calling him "technically reactionary" and "old-fashioned"? (Presumably, this is how these critics hope to show they are not behaving like stodgy cultural commissars.) I wouldn't call Bergman old-fashioned. But, despite some brilliant narrative inventions in his two best films, *The Silence* and *Persona*, his work doesn't suggest any fruitful development. He is an obsessional artist, the worst kind to imitate. Like Stein and Bacon and Jancscó, Bergman is one of those oppressively memorable geniuses of the artistic dead end, who go very far with a limited material—refining it when they are inspired, repeating it and parodying themselves when they aren't.

Interviewer: Many people have observed the "scandalous" fact that the sentiment of being for most great artists has been decidedly conservative, that their attachment to the past has been much more passionate than their feeling for things yet to be. Is there something about works of art which almost demands that their creators have a preservative, therefore conservative, relation to the world in which they live, even when committed to this or that "radical" policy. Perhaps in this sense art itself, whatever the artist's personal politics, is objectively conservative, therefore reactionary . . .

Sontag: "Reactionary" again! This feels like another version of the same question, so I'll try to answer in a different way. I doubt that there is anything more conservative or reactionary about artists than there is about people. And why shouldn't people be naturally conservative? That the past necessarily weighs more on the axis of human consciousness is perhaps a greater liability to the individual than to society, but how could it be otherwise? Where is the scandal? To be scandalized by the normal is always demagogic. And it is only normal that we are aware of ourselves as persons in a historical continuum, with indefinite thicknesses of past behind us, the present a razor's edge, and the future—well, problematic is one damp word for it. Dividing time into Past, Present, and Future suggests that reality is distributed equally among three parts, but in fact the past is the most real of all. The future is, inevitably, an accumulation of loss, and dying is something we do all our lives. If artists are memory specialists, professional curators of consciousness, they are only practicing—willfully, obsessionally—a prototypical devoutness. There is a tilt in the very experience of living which always gives memory an advantage over amnesia.

To reproach artists for having an insufficiently radical relation to the world has to be a complaint about art as such. And to reproach art is, in more than one way, like reproaching consciousness itself for being a burden. For consciousness can be conscious of itself, as Hegelians quaintly say, only through its sense of the past. And art is the most general condition of the Past in the present. To become past is, in one version, to become art. (The arts that most literally illustrate this mutation are architecture and photography.) The pathos that all works of art reek of comes from their historicity. From the way they are overtaken by physical decay and stylistic obsolescence. And from whatever is mysterious, partly (and forever) veiled about them. And simply from our awareness, with each work, that no one would or could ever do exactly *that* again. Perhaps no work of art *is* art. It can only *become* art, when it is part of the past. In this normative sense, a "contemporary" work of art would be a contradiction—except so far as we can, in the present, assimilate the present to the past.

Interviewer: And yet a great many contemporary liberationists, radicals of various kinds, have demanded that works of art be new, that they cut loose from the inherited props and furnishings of the familiar material world.

Sontag: But wouldn't that be like peeling off one's own skin? And doesn't demanding that artists throw away their toys—that is, the world—mean wanting them not to be artists anymore? Such a talent for jettisoning everything has to be extremely rare. And its promised benefits have yet to be demonstrated. The clean sweep being proposed as a goal for radical therapy as well as art (and, by extension, for politics) suggests that "liberation" can be very confining. That is, it seems regressive in relation to the full range of our possibilities—among which civilization tries, to almost everyone's dissatisfaction, to arbitrate. The price we would pay for liberation in that undialectical sense is at least as steep as the price we've been paying for civilization. If we are indeed going to be forced to choose between defensive fantasies of liberation and ruling corruptions of civilization, let's work fast to soften the harshness of that choice. It's sobering to realize that both options seemed just as morally defective a century ago when Henry James made his prescient, melancholy analysis of our post-1960s cultural dilemmas in *The Princess Casamassima*, with imaginary London anarchists anticipating American New Left and countercultural ideologues.

You seem to be talking about a politicized version of the classic modernist demand on Art (Making It New), but then the only difference between the Poundian demand and the more recent imperatives is a radical politics, and

I'm not sure that the language in which this politics is declared should be taken at face value. Question the self-designated radicals who appear to be calling for a cultural tabula rasa, and I think you'd find that they are seldom as modernist as their rhetoric would imply. The way you've formulated their protest seems to me to confuse a moralistic political radicalism (assumed to be a Good Thing) with an amoral revolt against the inherited past that is in full complicity with the status quo. Much of radical dissent is animated by a kind of restorationism—the wish to reconstitute communal pleasures and civic virtues that have been wiped out to make possible the very real tabula rasa of our consumer society. A radical in the sense you describe would be Andy Warhol, the ideally passive avatar of an economy in which everything of the past is scheduled to be traded in for newer goods.

Interviewer: What do you make of this assertion by the sociologist Philip Rieff: "Never before has there been such a general shifting of sides as now among intellectuals in the United States and England. Many have gone over to the enemy without realizing that they, self-considered the cultural elite, have actually become spokesmen for what Freud called the instinctual [mass]." Insofar as some of your own work in the mid-sixties attempted to legitimate an easier relation between popular culture and the elite, would you say that you had "gone over to the enemy"?

Sontag: [Laughter]

Interviewer: What?

Sontag: Of course I wouldn't say that.

Interviewer: Well, do you think it is useful to draw a distinction between "the cultural elite" and "the instinctual mass"?

Sontag: No. I think the distinction is a vulgar one. By ignoring the difference between the descriptive and prescriptive senses of culture, it can't give a properly specific meaning to either. There are several senses in which "culture" doesn't equal "elite." (Anyway, there are elites—not one, but many.) And I don't think that "instinctual" and "mass" go together—even if Le Bon and Freud did say so. The distinction suggests a contempt for the instincts, a facile pessimism about people, and a lack of passion for the arts (as distinct from ideas) that is not confirmed by my own instincts, pessimism, passions.

Intellectuals who want to defend our poor sick culture should resist the all-too-understandable temptation to fume about the unlettered masses and accuse other intellectuals of joining the enemy. If I'm leery of talking about a cultural elite, it's not because I don't care about culture but because I think the notion is virtually unusable and should be retired. For instance, it doesn't explain anything about the cultural mix I was writing about in the mid-sixties— a particularly vivid moment in a century-long set of exchanges between different levels of culture, different elites. Early modernists like Rimbaud, Stravinsky, Apollinaire, Joyce, and Eliot had showed how "high culture" could assimilate shards of "low culture" (*The Waste Land*, *Ulysses*, etc., etc.). By the 1960s the popular arts, notably film and rock music, had taken up the abrasive themes and some of the "difficult" techniques (like collage) that had hitherto been the fare of a restricted cultural elite, if you will—the university-educated, museum-going cosmopolitan audience for the avant-garde or experimental arts. That low culture was an important ingredient in the modernist takeover of high culture, that the modernist sensibility had created new boundaries for popular culture and was eventually incorporated into it—these are subjects that nobody who has cared for culture can ignore or should fail to treat with high seriousness. Is trying to understand something—in this instance, a process that had been going on at least since Baudelaire—legitimizing it? It hardly needed me to offer that legitimacy. And the 1960s seems rather late to stop identifying culture with some Masterpiece Theatre of World History and to respond—on the basis of contemporary experience, and moved by pleasure rather than resentment—to how complex the destiny of high culture has become since Matthew Arnold whistled in the dark on Dover Beach. The notion of culture implied by Rieff's distinction seems to me awfully middlebrow, and plausible only to someone who has never been really immersed in or derived intense pleasure from contemporary poetry and music and painting. Does culture here mean art? (And what art?) Does it mean thought? They're not the same, and culture isn't exactly synonymous with either. Toryish labels like "cultural elite" and "instinctual mass" do not tell us anything useful about how to protect that endangered species, "high" standards. Diagnoses of cultural sickness made in such general and self-congratulatory terms become a symptom of the problem, not part of the answer.

Interviewer: In 1964, in your essay "Notes on Camp," you wrote: "I am strongly drawn to camp, and almost as strongly offended by it. That is why I want to talk about it, and why I can." And you continued: "To name a sensibility, to draw its contours and to recount its history, requires a deep sympathy modified by revulsion." Could you tell us something more about that dual set of attitudes—sympathy/revulsion—particularly in relation to what you call "the corny flamboyance of femaleness" embodied in certain actresses? And how do such responses relate to your feminist sensibility?

Sontag: Like the recent essays on photography, "Notes on Camp" grew out of speculations of a rather general order. How "to name a sensibility," how "to draw its contours, to recount its history"—that was the problem I started from, and then looked for an example, a model. And it seemed more interesting not to pick Sensibility X from among those heaped with ethical or aesthetic laurels, and to evoke instead a sensibility that was exotic and in obvious ways minor, even despised—as the rather quirky notion of a sensibility had itself been slighted, in favor of that tidier fiction, an "idea."

Morbidity was my first choice. I stayed with that for a while, attempting to systematize a long-term fascination with mortuary sculpture, architecture, inscriptions, and other such wistful lore that eventually found an unsystematic place in *Death Kit* and *Promised Lands*. But the material was too detailed, and cumbersome to describe, so I switched to camp, which had the advantage of being familiar as well as marginal, and could be illustrated in a more rapid and comprehensible way. Camp, I knew, was a sensibility that many people were tuned in to, although they might have no name for it. As for myself: by deciding to write "Notes on Camp" instead of "Notes on Death," I was choosing to humor the part of my seriousness that was being zapped and loosened up and made more sociable by camp wit, rather than to fortify the part of my wit that got regularly choked off by seizures of morbidity. Compared to morbidity, camp was hard to pin down. It was, in fact, a rich example of how a sensibility can have divergent meanings, can have a latent content that is more complex than—and often different from—its manifest one.

Which brings me to the question of ambivalence. I've dawdled in the culture graveyard, enjoying what camp taste could effect in the way of ironic resurrections, just as I've stopped to pay my respects to real death, in real cemeteries, off the country roads and in the cities of three continents. And it is in the nature of such detours that some sights fascinate, while others repel. The theme you single out—the parodistic rendering of women—usually left me cold. But I can't say that I was simply offended. For I was often amused and, so far as I needed to be, liberated. I think that the camp taste for the theatrically feminine did help undermine the credibility of certain stereotyped femininities—by exaggerating them, by putting them between quotation marks. Making something corny of femaleness is one way of creating distance from the stereotype. Camp's extremely sentimental relation to beauty is no help to women, but its irony is: ironizing about the sexes is one small step toward depolarizing them. In this sense the diffusion of camp taste in the early sixties should probably be credited with a considerable if inadvertent role in the upsurge of feminist consciousness in the late 1960s.

Interviewer: What about women like Mae West, an old-style sex queen who didn't, apparently, strike audiences the way you suggest?

Sontag: I think she did. Whether or not she started with the oldest of blandishments, her glory was as a new-style sex queen—that is, the impersonator of one. Unlike Sarah Bernhardt's style, which audiences at a certain moment stopped being able to take straight, Mae West's was appreciated from the beginning as a sort of parody. Letting oneself, self-consciously, be beguiled by such robust, shrill, vulgar parody is the last step in a century-long evolution—and progressive democratization—of the aestheticism whose broader history and implications are sketched in "Notes on Camp" but which has had its most knowing reception from the milieu in which the word "camp" appeared some fifty years ago. (Although scholars of slang disagree as much about the origin of "camp" as they do about "O.K.," I assume that it derives from *camper*—which the Oxford French Dictionary translates as "to posture boldly.") And it was in the 1920s that a kind of deconstruction of the stereotypes of femininity gets underway, a mocking challenge to sexism that complements the moralistic call for justice and reparations to women that had found its voice in the 1890s in, say, Shaw's essays and George Gissing's novel *The Odd Women*. What I am arguing is that today's feminist consciousness has a long and complicated history, of which the diffusion of male homosexual taste is a part—including its sometimes witless put-downs of and delirious homage to the "feminine." Feminists have been less quick at seeing this than some of their opponents— for example, Wyndham Lewis, whose novel-diatribe *The Childermass*, written in the late twenties, contains a long speech about how the naturally feminine and the masculine are being subverted jointly by homosexuals and by suffragettes. (Contemporary homosexuality is denounced as "a branch of the Feminist Revolution.") And Lewis was not wrong to link them.

Interviewer: In "The Pornographic Imagination," written in 1967, you describe the heroine of *Story of O* as a woman who "progresses simultaneously toward her own extinction as a human being and her fulfillment as a sexual being." You then wonder "how anyone would ascertain whether there exists, truly, empirically, anything in 'nature' or human consciousness that supports such a split." It seems to me that the loss of self in exchange for sexual fulfillment might be viewed as an allegory of the new feminist awareness. That is, in exchange for "fulfillment as women," women have often surrendered their identities as autonomous individuals. Do you agree there might be more to *Story of O* than you saw in 1967? Could that book be considered a peculiarly political work whose meaning could be enriched by the feminist perspective?

Sontag: Though I'd agree that one can extract useful lessons from all sorts of unpromising material, O's destiny seems to me an unlikely allegory of either feminist awareness or, simply, the age-old subjection of women. My interest in *Story of O* was, still would be, in its candor about the demonic side of sexual fantasy. The violence of the imagination that it consecrates—and does not at all deplore—cannot be confined within the optimistic and rationalist perceptions of mainstream feminism. Pornography's form of utopistic thinking is, like most of science fiction, a negative utopia. Since the writers who have insisted on how fierce, disruptive, and antinomian an energy sexuality (potentially, ideally) is are mostly men, it's commonly supposed that this form of the imagination must discriminate against women. I don't think it does, necessarily. (It could discriminate against men, as in Monique Wittig's celebrations of unfettered sexual energy.)

What distinguishes the work of "the pornographic imagination" from other accounts of the erotic life is that it treats sexuality as an extreme situation. That means that what pornography depicts is, in one obvious sense, quite unrealistic. Sexual energy is not endlessly renewable; sex acts cannot be tirelessly repeated. But in another sense pornography is rudely accurate about important realities of desire. That voluptuousness does mean surrender, and that sexual surrender pursued imaginatively enough, experienced immoderately enough, does erode pride of individuality and mocks the notion that the will could ever be free—these are truths about sexuality itself and what it may, naturally, become. Because it is such an *ascesis* to live completely for voluptuousness, only a few women and men ever do pursue pleasure to this terminal extreme. The fantasy of sexual apocalypse is common enough, however—indisputably, a means for intensifying sexual pleasure. And what that tells us about the inhuman, as it were, character of intense pleasure is still being slighted by the humanist "revisionist" Freudianism that most feminists feel comfortable with, which minimizes the intractable powers of unconscious or irrational feeling.

You propose a political view of the book in place of my tentative idea about something "in 'nature,' or in human consciousness." But I would still reaffirm that speculation. There seems to be something inherently defective or self-frustrating in the way the sexual impulse works in human beings—for instance, an essential (that is, normal), not accidental (that is, neurotic), link between sexual energy and obsession. It appears likely that the full development of our sexual being does clash with the full development of our consciousness. Instead of supposing that *all* our sexual discontent is part of a tax sexuality pays for being civilized, it may be more correct to assume that we are, first of all, sick by nature—and that it is our being, to begin with, what Nietzsche called "sick animals," that makes us civilization-producing animals.

It is the innate incongruence between important achievements in the realms of sexual fulfillment and of individual consciousness that is exacerbated by the enlarged use to which sexuality has been put in modern, secular culture. As the credibility of religious experience has declined, erotic experience has not only gotten an inflated, even grandiose significance, but is itself now subjected to standards of credibility (thereby attaching a whole new sort of anxiety to sexual performance). In particular, the quest for the experience of complete psychic surrender now no longer enclosed within traditional religious forms has become increasingly, and restlessly, attached to the mind-blowing character of the orgasm. The myths of total sexual fulfillment dramatized in *Story of O* concern that peculiarly modern *via negativa*. Evidence about the feelings and sexual tastes in our culture before it was wholly secularized, and in other cultures past and present, suggests that voluptuousness was rarely pursued in this way, as the organon to transcend individual consciousness. Perhaps only when sexuality is invested with that ideological burden, as it is now, does it also become a real, and not just a potential, danger to personhood and to individuation.

Interviewer: In his book *Fellow Teachers*, Philip Rieff writes: "True criticism is constituted, first, by repeating what is already known. The great teacher is he who, because he carries in himself what is already known, can transfer it to his student; that inwardness is his absolute and irreducible authority. If a student fails to recognize that authority, then he is not a student." Obviously, the authoritative knowing Rieff invokes has nothing to do with

the expertise of the specialist. What do you take him to
mean by it, and would you agree that, according to Rieff's
definition, there are very few students in our institutions
of higher learning?

Sontag: Precious few students, according to that
definition—yes. But perhaps still more than enough,
since—again following Philip Rieff's definition—there are
probably *no* professors. The authority of the professoriat
being invoked here goes no further back than Wilhel-
mine Germany. That there are very few students in the
prescriptive sense (devoted, talented lovers of learning) is
surely as well known as that there are many more students
in the descriptive sense (bodies in classrooms), liberal-arts
education having assumed those functions which, precisely, make it harder than it was a generation ago to as-
sign so-called difficult books and to expound complex ideas
without back talk from students. But Philip Rieff does not
make his case against mass education more convincing by
overstating it. When in Western intellectual history did
the college teacher have "an absolute and irreducible authority"? Even in the great ages of faith, which one might
suppose well-stocked with models for the pedagogue as
dictator, a closer look discloses a reassuring ferment of
dissent, of heterodoxy, of questioning what was "already
known." Fiat cannot restore to the office of the teacher
(now irrevocably secular, transmitting a plurality of "traditions") an absolute authority that both the teacher and
what is being taught do not have—if they ever did.

The genuine historical pressures to lower the standards for higher learning that do exist aren't weakened by declaring what words *ought* to mean—defining a teacher as one who teaches authoritatively, a student as one who accepts the authority of the teacher. Perhaps one should take Philip Rieff's definitions as evidence that the fight to maintain the highest standards really is a lost cause. If the decline of first-rate teaching in universities really is irreversible, as it probably is, then one should expect exactly such a defense of the *ancien régime* as is projected by these empty definitions of great teacher and great student. Making a virtue of its own historical inappropriateness, Philip Rieff's authoritarian theory of the university parallels the authoritarian theory of the bourgeois state advanced in Germany and France in the late nineteenth and early twentieth centuries. Whereas, traditionally, a teacher had authority by virtue of a particular doctrine, a "teaching," what is proposed here is a very modern, contentless notion of authority: not the authority of, say, the Nicene Creed, but the authority of—authority. The substance of the teacher's authority having been eroded, only its form remains. Authority itself ("that inwardness") is made the defining characteristic of the great teacher. Perhaps one only stakes out such a large, truculent claim to authority when one doesn't, can't possibly, have it. Even in the Maoist conception of the relation between leaders and masses, the authority of the Great Teacher does not derive, tautologically, from his authority, but from his wisdom—a much-advertised part of which consists in overturning "what is already known." But Philip Rieff's notion of the teacher has more in common with the Maoist pedagogic conception than with the main tradition of Western activity and high culture that he thinks he's defending against barbarous students: it is formulated in a fashion as dismissive of independence of thought as Maoism.

To define a teacher primarily in terms of the idea of authority seems to me grossly inadequate to the standards of that elite education for which Philip Rieff is proselytizing. That the definition encourages wishful thinking and licenses personal arrogance is relatively unimportant. What is important is that it leaves out virtually all the teacherly virtues. Wisdom, as I've already mentioned. And the Socratic pedagogic eros. Forget about humility—if that is too radical, or it sounds mawkish. But what about skepticism?

A little skepticism about what one "carries" in oneself, if one is well-educated, might be especially useful—to balance the temptations of self-righteousness. As someone who, like Philip Rieff, had the good fortune to do undergraduate work in the most ambitious and the most successful authoritarian program of education ever devised in this country—the Hutchins-era College of the University of Chicago—I remain as much as he, I would think, a partisan of the nonelective curriculum. But I'm aware that all such forms of consensus about "great" books and "perennial" problems, once stabilized, tend to deteriorate eventually into something philistine. The real life of the mind is always at the frontiers of "what is already known."

Those great books don't only need custodians and trans-
mitters. To stay alive, they also need adversaries. The
most interesting ideas are heresies.

Interviewer: I would like to link "The Pornographic
Imagination" with your essay on Riefenstahl, where you
discuss the aesthetics of totalitarian art. To what extent is
Story of O a totalitarian work? Or an ironic commentary
upon such a work? Is there a connection between this tale
of total female submission and Riefenstahl's work, with its
focus on obeisance to an all-powerful leader?

Sontag: I don't find *Story of O* ironic, either about totalitarianism or about the Sadean literary tradition of which
it is a self-conscious but exquisitely limited moderniza-
tion. Is it a totalitarian work? The connection that could
be drawn between *Story of O* and the eroticized politics
of Nazism seems a fortuitous one—and extraneous to
the book and the intentions of the woman who wrote it,
pseudonymously—however easily it springs to mind now,
especially since the sadomasochistic dramaturgy started
going in for Nazi drag. And there is still another difference worth noting, the one between the eroticism of a
political event (real or, say, in a film) and the eroticism of
a private life (real or fictional). Hitler, when he used sexual metaphors to express the authority of leaders and the
obeisance of masses, in characterizing leadership as viola-
tion could only *compare* the masses to a woman. (But O *is*
one woman, and the book is about an individual salvation,
through the erotic, which is profoundly anti-political, as
all forms of mysticism and neo-mysticism are.) Measured

against submission and fulfillment in a real erotic situation, the eroticism of Hitler's notion of leadership (as rape) and of followership (as surrender) is a cheat, a fake.

As there is a difference between an idea, mediated by a metaphor, and an experience (real or fictional), the metaphors used by the modern regimes that have sought to create total ideological consensus have different degrees of closeness to or distance from practical reality. In the communist view of how leaders lead masses, the metaphor is one not of sexual domination but of teachership: the teacher who has authority and the masses who are students of the teacher. Although this metaphor makes Maoist rhetoric very attractive, almost as attractive as Nazi rhetoric is repellent, its result is probably a much more total system of control over minds and bodies. While the eroticized politics of fascism is, after all, a pseudo-eroticism, the pedagogic politics of communism is a real and effective process of teaching.

Interviewer: In 1965, you wrote an essay on science-fiction films called "The Imagination of Disaster."* Have you reflected about science fiction since then—for example, about the idea of intelligence proposed in Arthur Clarke's *Childhood's End?* Can you make a connection between "the imagination of disaster" and "the pornographic imagination"? And between leaders and followers in fascist aesthetics?

Sontag: That essay, among others, could be seen as one

* In *Against Interpretation*, Farrar, Straus and Giroux, 1966.

phase of an argument about modes of authoritarian feeling and perception. (And the argument isn't only to be found in my essays. For instance, *Duet for Cannibals* and *Brother Carl*, the two films I made in Sweden, and two recent stories, "Old Complaints Revisited" and "Doctor Jekyll," are fictional treatments of the private lives of leaders and followers.) Science fiction—about which I hope to write a better essay someday—is full of authoritarian ideas, ideas that have much in common with those developed in other contemporary contexts (like pornography), illustrating typical forms of the authoritarian imagination. Clarke's fable is one of the abler examples of science fiction's characteristic polemic on behalf of an authoritarian ideal of intelligence. The romantic protest against the assassin mind, a leading theme of art and thought since the early nineteenth century, gradually became a self-fulfilling prophecy as, in the twentieth century, technocratic, purely instrumental ideas of the mind took over, which made intelligence seem hopelessly inadequate to a social and psychological disorder experienced as more menacing than ever. Science fiction promotes the idea of a superior or "higher" intelligence that will impose order on human affairs and messy emotions and, thereby, end childhood—that is, history. Pornography, like the fascist mass spectacle, looks to the abolition of mind (in an ideal choreography of bodies, of dominators and the dominated).

We live in a culture in which intelligence is denied relevance altogether, in a search for radical innocence, or is defended as an instrument of authority and repression. In my view, the only intelligence worth defending is critical, dialectical, skeptical, desimplifying. An intelligence which aims at the definitive resolution (that is, suppression) of conflict, which justifies manipulation—always, of course, for other people's good, as in the argument brilliantly made by Dostoevsky's Grand Inquisitor, which haunts the main tradition of science fiction—is not *my* normative idea of intelligence. Not surprisingly, contempt for intelligence goes with the contempt for history. And history is, yes, tragic. But I'm not able to support any idea of intelligence which aims at bringing history to an end—substituting for the tragedy that makes civilization at least possible the nightmare or the Good Dream of eternal barbarism.

I am assuming that the defense of civilization implies the defense of an intelligence that is not authoritarian. But all contemporary defenders of civilization must be aware—though I don't think it helps to say it often—that this civilization, already so far overtaken by barbarism, *is* at an end, and nothing we do will put it back together again. So, in the culture of transition out of which we can try to make sense, fighting off the twin afflictions of hyper-aesthesia and passivity, no position can be a comfortable one or should be complacently held. Perhaps the most instructive discussion of the questions of intelligence and innocence, civilization and barbarism, responsibility to the truth and responsibility to people's needs, is in the libretto of Schönberg's *Moses and Aaron*. Dostoevsky does not let Jesus answer the Grand Inquisitor's monologue, although the whole novel is supposed to give us, does give us, the material to construe that answer. But Moses and Aaron do answer each other's arguments. And although Schönberg uses both dramaturgy and music to stack the whole opera against the view Aaron represents, and for the Word of Moses, in the actual debate between them he set their arguments at parity. So the debate is unresolved, as it really is, for these questions are fiercely complicated. Moses and Aaron are both right. And any serious argument about culture—which has to be, finally, an argument about truth—must honor that complexity.

(1975)

Acknowledgments

"The Double Standard of Aging" first appeared in *The Saturday Review*, September 23, 1972, and was later published in *Susan Sontag: Essays of the 1960s & 70s* (Library of America, 2013).

"The Third World of Women" first appeared in *The Partisan Review* 40, no. 2 (Spring 1973), and was later published in *Susan Sontag: Essays of the 1960s & 70s* (Library of America, 2013).

"A Woman's Beauty: Put-Down or Power Source?" and "Beauty: How Will It Change Next?" first appeared in *Vogue*, in April and May 1975, respectively, and were later published in *Susan Sontag: Essays of the 1960s & 70s* (Library of America, 2013).

"Fascinating Fascism" first appeared in *The New York Review of Books*, February 6, 1975, and was later published in *A Susan Sontag Reader* (Farrar, Straus and Giroux, 1982). "Feminism and Fascism: An Exchange Between Adrienne Rich and Susan Sontag," written in response, first appeared in *The New York Review of Books*, March 20, 1975.

Acknowledgments

"The *Salmagundi* Interview" first appeared in the quarterly *Salmagundi*, no. 31–32 (Fall 1975–Winter 1976). It is a slightly abridged version of an interview conducted in April 1975 by Robert Boyars, editor of *Salmagundi*, and Maxine Bernstein. It was later published in *A Susan Sontag Reader* (Farrar, Straus and Giroux, 1982).